Praise for *Running from Miracles*

"Some people say there is no God, but you've come too late for me to believe that because I've felt his love, experienced his faithfulness and goodness, saw his beauty and miracles and I have walked with his angels. I love you and I pray that your book will be a blessing to you and to others and I pray that it will lead someone to know our loving Father and the hope that we always have in him. Love you, Momma"

–*Robin Decker*
Mother of Shawn Decker

"As I read through the pages of this book, I can remember some of the events and the way Shawn has come through them. There are two things that stick out to me. One is the never- ending grace and love of God for us all; and number two is the courage that Shawn has shown in the dark times to keep going. I have been encouraged and motivated to start again by this book. I pray as you read this book, let God show you the way out as He has shown Shawn. I am very proud of the Man of God you have become, and He isn't done yet! Let's all reach for the higher goals in life."

–*Dr. A.E.Crabtree*
President of Eddie Crabtree Ministries
and Senior Pastor of Valley Word Church

"This book is a great read about real life. In his transparency, Shawn has shared his vulnerability. Yet in being vulnerable Shawn has exhibited inner strength; a strength that only God can supply. This book reveals that God can perfect himself in imperfect people and can accomplish his will and purpose in our lives when we allow him to. For with God nothing shall be impossible (Luke 1:37)."

–Rev. Stephanie Long-Scott
Nothings Impossible Greeting Cards
www.nigreetings.com

"Shawn uses his own personal life stories to give readers a perfect view of God's unrelenting love. One message that impacted me was what Shawn shared about misplaced passion. He uses the example of how a fire in the living room fireplace brings warmth to the home, but that if that same fire was located on the living room floor it would burn the house down. He ends by saying that 'Passion not in its proper place can destroy your life.' That one example has challenged me to reevaluate many of my personal, business and ministry choices."

–Sandra Bird Aldridge, Minister
Who Will Go For Us

Running from Miracles

It's Time to Come Home

Shawn E. Decker

International
PUBLISHING, INC.

Chesapeake, Virginia

Editor: Emily Mowry
Cover Design & Layout: Patricia Goedeke

Printed in the United States of America.

International
PUBLISHING, INC.

Published by International Publishing Inc.
Chesapeake, VA

ISBN-13: 978-1-946917-07-2
ISBN-10: 1-946917-07-9

Scripture quotations throughout this book are taken from the Holy Bible, from the following translations: New King James Version, New International Version, The Message and New Living Translation.

Contact us at shawnedecker.com

First and foremost, I dedicate this book to God.
Without him, his love, and his constant sustaining Grace, I would have never been able
to make it through these things in my life. Secondly I thank God for my family, wife, sons,
and all the others that have brought both pain and pleasure to my life.
Because without them, I would not be the person that I am!

I would also like to give a special thanks to Dr. A.E. Crabtree for his teaching
because without it, the book would be an impossible feat to me at the time,
and I don't believe I would have ever had the courage to start!

Most importantly, I would like to thank my wife, Amanda Decker
for her ridiculous amount of patience with my lack of literacy, bad spelling,
horrible grammar, and my constant frustrations with my first book!
She has been a constant guide, steady hand, and always stood true,
even when she wanted to beat me black and blue.

Table of Contents

Foreword

I WAS TRULY HONORED when asked to write the foreword for this book. Shawn and I have been friends now for over ten years. My husband and I first met Shawn when he was assigned to do an appraisal on our house for a loan to refinance. He was a friendly, down to earth guy who immediately connected with us in general conversation and by the end of the appraisal, we had connected spiritually. It did not take long for us to discover that Shawn was a talker and once he discovered I was too, his initial purpose for visiting our home changed. Through questions he posed regarding the appraisal, I began sharing why we decided to refinance. Without hesitation, I enlightened him about our story and testimony of losing our first and second born sons to stillbirth, full term and almost a year a part. I am an individual who demonstrates radical faith and before you knew it, all three of us began testifying to the goodness of Jesus and all He had done for us. There we were three strangers, standing in tears, glorifying God together and instantly a friendship occurred. Not only did we share in our personal struggles and triumphs, but we also began sharing our individual passions, dreams and visions.

> *"For everything there is a season, a time for every activity under heaven."* –Ecclesiastes 3:1 (NLT)

One thing I do not believe in is coincidences. I believe God sets individuals in our paths for a reason some are for a season and some are for a lifetime. Through the years, it has become more apparent on that day, the Lord predestined the three of us to be standing together in my basement encouraging one another through His word. Upon Shawn's departure, we exchanged numbers and email addresses and began working together through our individual ministries. My husband Byron and I had been studying more about finances and breaking the curse of poverty. We were studying and focusing on biblical prosperity and how to see it manifested in every area of our lives. We had put together a workshop titled, *Breaking the Curse of Poverty* and discovered Shawn had been working on a workshop and series titled the *Power of Value*. I introduced him to my Pastor and the relationship expanded. He ended up hosting a workshop at my church and his *Power of Value* DVD remains to this day in the library of our church and school.

> *"So all of us who have had that veil removed can see and reflect the glory of the Lord. And the Lord—who is the Spirit—makes us more and more like him as we are changed into his glorious image."* –2 Corinthians 3:18 (NLT)

Through the years, we have watched one another grow stronger in the Lord. We both have become more knowledgeable of the Word of God and have become vessels for the Kingdom. Revelation 12:11, informs us that we overcome by the blood of the Lamb and the power of our testimony. It was our testimonies of faith and victory that connected us the day we met, it has been our testimonies of God's grace and mercy that has equipped us to aid others and position them for purpose and it has been the testimonies of God's daily miracles in our lives that led to the purpose of this book.

I remember reading a quote that states, "Your story is the key that can unlock someone else's prison." Being transparent is not something that people are eagerly willing to do. Most individuals are not diligently running to share their mistakes, to share their fears, to share their struggles, to share their doubts and sins. As a leader, I have learned transparency is respected by those you are trying to lead, and it makes you more relatable to people. Of course, all things must be done with wisdom and as believers, we must seek the Lord for discernment. Shawn is a man whose passion is to let his own life's story become a witness to others. He is not afraid to uncover his own setbacks and downfalls for the benefit of saving someone else from undergoing the same pain, misery and despair. I have always appreciated his honesty and genuineness as it is what connected us when we first met.

"Hope deferred makes the heart sick, but a dream fulfilled is a tree of life."–Proverbs 13:12 (NLT)

This book, *Running from Miracles* is a book of hope. So many people walk in defeat because their hope has been shattered. Life happens and the effects of it can leave you broken and feeling lost. Psalm 34:18 tells us, "The LORD is close to the brokenhearted; he rescues those whose spirits are crushed" (NLT). This book sheds light while providing hope to those who may feel they are in a hopeless situation. Our Heavenly Father longs for each of us to be in the right relationship with Him. When the cares of life weigh you down, you can easily lose focus and instead of drawing closer to our Creator, we can be driven farther away. No matter what state we are in, God is always there. He is omnipresent, He is omnipotent, he has unlimited power. Whether you are a believer or a non-believer, this book will inspire you. Through stories and testimonies, through life reflections and personal prayers, it will allow you to see the presence of God and how His unfailing love sustains and keeps us all even when we are unaware. It is the Lord's desire that we all return to Him.

- Elder Charnika Elliott, M.Ed.

"You have shown me the way of life, and you will fill me with the joy of your presence." Acts 2:28 (NLT)

Introduction

OF ALL THE THINGS I have learned in my life, the most important is that God disguises miracles. In fact, if you're not looking, you may just call it a coincidence. I have had a life full of "coincidences", but I have learned that miracles are only seen in the details.

I believe that God will use even some of the worst things that we have gone through for the good. Throughout the bible, I noticed that there are many times that God hid his people. While God was hiding them to protect them, these years were hard for them; they saw them as "desert years." Though the bible does not include details of these years, we know that they happened. I have seen "desert years" in my own and others' lives; just as God's people in the bible had dark years hidden in a cave, so do we. For much of this book, I will show you what I have seen God do in my dark and/or hidden years! I expose myself, but I do not condone the bad, wrong, or even horrible actions that I have seemingly done over and over. I aim to show the love, grace, mercy, and compassion of God that taught me lessons that I did not want to learn!

I am sure that there will be many stories about my life that will make you laugh, cry, and even motivate you. However, my real hope is that, as you read this book, it will inspire you to have hope, no matter what you are going through. I hope that my words will motivate you to give God a chance to work in your life because it is not over. It is only the beginning of the good life that He has for you, but it is a journey! Throughout my life, I have struggled with sexual addiction, pornography, bad relationships, depression, cutting, poor self-image, drugs, smoking, drinking, bankruptcy, divorce, estrangement from my son and wife, alienation, thoughts of suicide, anger, fighting, and sexual orientation. Then I learned about a loving God that I could rely on like never before. He was a God that was, and is, with me always, no matter where I am in life. And He will do the same with you!

> Gen 28:15 NIV ¹⁵ I am with you and will watch over you wherever you go, and I will bring you back to this land. I will not leave you until I have done what I have promised you.'

> Gen 28:15 MSG ¹⁵ Yes. I'll stay with you, I'll protect you wherever you go, and I'll bring you back to this very ground. I'll stick with you until I've done everything I promised you."

That same God that said these things to the Israelites has watched over me and watches over you. My hope is to impart the lessons I have learned throughout my life to you so that you might grow in your relationship with Christ, that you may see a God that loves you, and that you will stop *Running from Miracles* and run to the miracle maker!

I do not believe that there is one person in this world that cannot relate to some part of this book. After every insightful, horrible, inspiring, terrifying, terrific, compelling part of my life, I spent the time to think about what I had learned. My hope is that you would do the same thing after reading this book.

CHAPTER 1

Looking for God

HAVE YOU EVER FELT like God was right there, even though you didn't believe He was responsible for anything going on around you? Well, in 1 Kings 19:11-13 (NKJV), it says there was "some wind, but God was not in it"; "an earthquake, but God was not in it"; "a fire, but God was not in it." But the "still small voice", He *was* in!

¹¹ Then He said, "Go out, and stand on the mountain before the LORD." And behold, the LORD passed by, and a great and strong wind tore into the mountains and broke the rocks in pieces before the LORD, but the LORD was not in the wind; and after the wind an earthquake, but the LORD was not in the earth-quake; ¹² and after the earthquake a fire, but the LORD was not in the fire; and after the fire a still small voice.

¹³ So it was, when Elijah heard it, that he wrapped his face in his mantle and went out and stood in the entrance of the cave. Suddenly a voice came to him, and said, "What are you doing here, Elijah?" (1 Kings 19:11-13, NKJV).

Later, in John 12, it says that Jesus was talking to the Father and God responded back to Jesus. Some said they heard thunder, others thought it was an angel, but Jesus said that "God responded audibly for [their] sake."

[28] *Father, glorify Your name." Then a voice came from heaven, saying, "I have both glorified it and will glorify it again." 29 Therefore the people who stood by and heard it said that it had thundered. Others said, "An angel has spoken to Him." 30 Jesus answered and said, "This voice did not come because of Me, but for your sake. (John 12:28-31, NKJV)*

I heard Jesse Duplantis, a Christian Minister, say that "People do not run from God; they run from what God has called them to do" (Duplantis, nd). Many times, I believe God shows us His love and mercy in certain situations, but we do not see it because we are looking for the spectacular and not the supernatural. Throughout this book, I am going to expose myself and some of my most intimate thoughts, actions, and mistakes. I will also share some of the perceptions that I had in my life. I will talk about the many miracles that have both happened to me, around me, and through me in the various stages of my life. Hopefully this will open your eyes to see how God is having an impact on and in your life. As you read every story, you will begin to see how God is working in and through you in so many different ways, situations, people, circumstances, and even events. Maybe you are missing the miracle that is right before you!

Another saying I have heard is, "The teacher is always silent during the test". He has taught us and given us the answer, but it is our job to pay attention to the master so that we can pass the test. Most of the tests that we go through are not worth taking twice. As long as we are paying attention, we don't have to take the test twice. God is to us as a parent is to their children. A child will go to pick something up, but they are still too small to actually pick it up. So the parent grabs the other side of the heavy load and assists the child. Then the child looks happily at the parent saying,

"Look mom, look dad, I did it!"

And the parent, because of their love, looks at their child and says,

"That's right, you did it, baby."

To build confidence, children need to tackle the bigger things in life. Much of the time, God is the same way. To me, this is not just a personal testimony but a testament of the love and generosity of my Savior. He is such a loving and caring father. Many times I think that we look at our earthly relationships and assume that Father God is the same way. However, I have a testimony of his overwhelming goodness, so let me tell you about My Jesus!

CHAPTER 2

A Little about My Mom
and Her Past:
Told from Her Perspective

WE BECOME WHO WE are through our experiences and the experiences of those that influence us. For most, the biggest influencers on our lives are our parents. I would like to introduce you to mine so that you can see where I came from. The following sections were created from interviews with my parents, Bill and Robin.

Robin's Story

As I stood in church singing praises to the Lord, my eyes closed and my hands lifted up singing the old hymn "I'll Fly Away". My mind went back fifty years to a small shotgun house on a southern cotton plantation that had been turned into a country church in Louisiana. The year was 1965. The sixties was a turbulent time, including events like the Vietnam War and violent protests associated with civil rights movements.

John F. Kennedy, Robert Kennedy, and Martin Luther King had all been assassinated. But there in the humid summer air, I remembered happy days of ongoing childhood, running from my cousins house through the woods to my great grandmother's house. It was a child's heaven. My whole family lived in those shotgun houses (so named because you could stand in the front door and shoot a shotgun all the way through the house).

I loved to stay on the farm with my grandparents. I would watch my grandmother make butter, homemade biscuits, and hot cocoa for breakfast. Then we would follow her around to feed the chickens, dogs, and milk the cows. She would try to let us milk them, but we were never quite able to master the art. After all our chores were finished, we would run and play in the corn and cotton fields. It would not always stay that way. Our innocence was stolen. After that, it was as if a dark fog settled over the swamp and the bayous, and my happy childhood days began to change. We don't ever talk about what happened to cause this change.

Mama's voice that once sang hymns changed to sobs. Daddy had always worked hard, but he had a weakness for women. And when mama found out, she became depressed and hysterical, threatening suicide and often took to bed for days at a time. Even though I was a child, I would often have to hide the knives and razors and empty the pills. I put sugar in the pills instead of medicine so that she would not overdose.

My dad was gone a lot because of work and other things. The days of going to church, having picnics after ball games, and swimming began to disappear. I was left to take care of things that were meant for adults. I was forced to grow up too quickly.

When I became a teenager, my dad had another affair. Mama started adding alcohol to her regimen of Valium. She went through another breakdown, and I started assuming more and more adult responsibilities. Even though I didn't have a driver's license yet, I was still too young. I would run errands in that small town, pay bills, help buy groceries, and other errands that Mama needed. My two older brothers were rebelling like a lot of the other younger people during the seventies. We saw the dishonesty of our government with the Vietnam War. The hippy movement was going strong with Woodstock music and smoking pot. We rebelled against the authority that told us not to do things that they themselves were doing. My brothers and I smoked pot and drank Boone's Farm® Wine. My brothers started drinking more and more and became wild, reckless, and angry. There were DUI's, wrecks, and confrontations with the police. Sometimes Mama and I would even have to physically try and hold them down to keep them from going crazy and grabbing a gun to go shoot someone. This would later cause my brother Dale to be shot in the back at a bar, and I would get to see him buried way too early in life.

A Lesson Learned

I have heard it said that unforgiveness is like drinking poison and expecting the other person to die! My mom told me later in life that she would have the opportunity to meet the man that killed her brother and tell him that she forgave him. This was something that has always encouraged me. No matter what I went through, I could find the strength to forgive anyone, no matter what!

Prayer

Father God, I ask you to give me the grace and strength to forgive others like you have forgiven me. To show me where I have chosen to not forgive others and to help me to correct that in my life.

CHAPTER 3

Mom, Dad
and How they Met

INTERVIEWING MY PARENTS on how they met led to many squabbles over the accuracy of facts. However, it truly happened, and they are still together today to tell the stories. Where one leaves off the other usually picks up the story.

Robin:

When I was eighteen, not quite nineteen, my dad was drinking really badly, and he needed a designated driver for him to drink out at a nightclub. By then, I had been involved with a guy and gotten pregnant, and I had a little girl, Nikki, who was two. That particular night my dad needed someone to drive him because he was drinking. He was the superintendent of an oil company in that area; most of the guys in that area either knew of him or worked for him. So a lot of the guys never would ask me out because of my dad and who he was.

I had known of your dad, Bill, for several years. He worked

for the oil company for my dad. The guy that I was involved with and lived with was Steven. It was a really rocky time being with him, but Bill would come to the door sometimes and knock to get Steven to go to work. Your dad was also working at my dad's camp, remodeling and fixing it. He used to hunt and fish with my brother Benny. Steven left when Nikki was only three months old. So then I would see your dad over like at my brother Benny's hunting, or at Gene's (Bills good friend). I would sometimes go to Billy and Gene's house, and he would be there hunting or fishing and I would see him for a minute. But he was involved with a woman at that time.

Bill:

I got out of the service in 1974 and went to Louisiana. I had been dating a girl Joan a year after I had gotten out of the service. She really enjoyed drinking so I was drunk most of the time. I don't remember all the ins and outs, but we met at a bar and we kind of hooked up. I moved in with her for a while. Then, I ended up in the hospital with bleeding ulcers. At the time, I had two or three thousand dollars in the bank. We drank that up, and back then beer was like fifty cents a bottle. We both drank beer and she drank up all the savings she had. I got just tired of how every time we did something, we would have to be drinking, so that's kind of what split us up, in a sense. She was terribly jealous. She carried a Berretta around in her purse and on several occasions had intentions of using it.

Although we had met, I first started noticing Robin after she had Nikki. Robin told me it embarrassed her the first time that I really remember seeing her with Nikki. She was holding

Nikki when she was just a baby and Nikki was teething on a venison bone. Kids loved to chew on them, and I didn't really notice it, but she was all dirty. Her face was covered in Barbecue sauce. She had been on the ground and she was dirty and dusty. While I was growing up, I had been around twenty-six nieces and nephews so I didn't even notice, but she said it had embarrassed her.

Robin:

On the first night that I called our first meeting, it was the first time that we actually talked for real and was the night after he had broken up with his girlfriend Joan. I was supposed to chauffeur for my daddy that night because he was drinking. So I took my daddy to this club, and they had music and dancing and all this other stuff. I took daddy in and he tells the bouncer "this is my daughter" and the bouncer is like "yeah, right Joe" because he had so many women he was involved with that the bouncer didn't believe him. Daddy was dancing and carrying on and I was only eighteen or nineteen years old at the time.

I was sitting in a corner drinking coke, watching my dad carrying on. I see Bill out there dancing. He's pretty lit by now, but he's having a good time. He had a fight with his girlfriend and had gone out. So he came over and asked me to dance; most of the guys that worked for my dad never asked me to dance or do anything because of who my daddy was. But he did, and, man he really could dance. When he had left that night, I had left and took my daddy home. Bill went to another bar where he got in a fight over someone else sitting on his bar stool. That guy called the law so he left and got stopped, got a

DUI, and got thrown in jail.

Bill:

That should have told me something right there, I met her and then got thrown in jail. We had the best time dancing and everything and something that we argued about for the next thirty years is how that night actually ended.

Robin:

I was pretty sure that he said, "I'm going to call you Friday, will you go out with me?", and I said yes. So I waited for him to call, but he never called. A couple weeks later, I did see him again, in my brother's yard. It was New Year's Eve, and he asked me if I would like to go out that night, and I said yes. And so we met that night and went out. That was our first official date, New Year's Eve 1978. He came and picked me up around eleven o'clock at night after he had gotten off work, and we went dancing and everything.

A Lesson Learned

Even when we have parents doing the complete wrong things, God can still be connecting us to the right people, navigating us to our destiny!

Prayer

Lord, I ask that you would help me to stay out of situations that I am not supposed to be in. Protect me from the situations I can't do anything about, and give me the wisdom to know the difference. Guide me and protect me so that I can experience the best you have for me!

CHAPTER 4

From First Date to Marriage

Robin:

FROM THAT FIRST DATE, we were literally inseparable. We saw each other every day. I was going to trade school during the day and college classes at night. Bill was commercial fishing during the day and working on an oil rig in the evening. During my lunch break at school, I would go over to his apartment and he would fix me lunch. Then at midnight when he got off work, he would come over and see me. From eleven o'clock at night until three or four in the morning, we would stay up and talk. A few hours later, I would go to school and he would go to work. He worked seven days a week for almost three years, but we would make time to have lunch together or something.

Most of the time, my daughter Nikki went with us everywhere. That was something that attracted me to him; he did not mind me bringing her along like most men did. I felt like she was a part of me, and if they didn't want to be around my child then, my thought was, really what was the use, you know? But he always was like: "well, of course." We were only dating a couple weeks, but I would go over to his house and we would smooch on the couch. I never will forget when he asked me to marry him. It was two weeks after our first date and he asked me to marry him. He said, "I'm gonna get married this summer, you wanna be my bride?" He said, "Before you answer, know I play for keeps." And that really meant something to me, that somebody really meant for good. So I said yes, and we had planned it for six months away. I was going to be a June bride.

I said yes, but every day that we dated we were going without sleep. Six months away seemed like such a long time. A month went by and we decided to just go ahead and get married. I planned on having a simple wedding of about forty people, but Bill would have anxiety attacks in crowds that exceeded about ten people. My family, mom and daddy, had a pretty nice house. It had a hall that led into a sunken living room with a double fireplace and a big cathedral-glass window. We were married in that room.

I just called some friends and said, "I'm getting married on Saturday, would you like to come?" There weren't any kind of invitations, there was like one spray of flowers, my bouquet, and some flowers for the table. We just had some punch and cake; and it was really cute because my flowers were yellow roses and daisies and my dress was yellow. For food, we just had cake and ice cream. That was because the day of the wedding, the bakery was supposed to deliver the wedding cake. When they delivered it, they had made a mistake and delivered clown cupcakes. I realized that should have been a bad omen, ya know. Mama was hysterically upset that they had delivered clown cupcakes, but I thought it was cool. I thought, well the kids will love it. Nikki was two when we got married, and she was our little flower girl.

What was cool about getting my wedding dress was that my dad did a lot of business with this one nice clothing shop. Daddy had a charge account there, and it was almost like a scene out of *Pretty Women*. Daddy was pretty well off and successful in his career. He had told me to go over to Mr. Sam's store (I think, I don't really remember the name of the store). He told me go over to Sam's and just get any dress I wanted and to tell him to put it on his charge account. Well, I was a pretty big tomboy back then, so I had on a flannel shirt, Levi jeans, and Dingo boots with no makeup and long hair. I went into the store and was looking at dresses and none of the sales ladies would come over and wait on me. I had found a really pretty light yellow dress that needed to be cut off because I'm so short at four feet eleven inches. When I went into Mr. Sam's office and said, "Mr. Sam, I'm getting married and I need this dress cut off, could you do something?" And oh he was hot that those women hadn't even waited on me. And of course, after, he made sure that the seamstress came to take care of me. That was kind of a funny story.

Bill woke up early as usual on our wedding day, got ready and had an eight pack of Miller ponies (beer). They were really short Millers. Then he went down to Jughead's and knocked on the door because he knew he also got up early. So they drank some more. In all, they drank about a fifth of Jack Daniels until it was time for him to get to the wedding. He had not told me he was going to do this, but he was doing it because he couldn't be around crowds of people. So at the wedding, I had warned everyone in my family "Y'all be good", because they could be a rowdy bunch. And I had told them that, "He's really quiet, so y'all be careful around him" and stuff. But when we got to the wedding, he came out and was like, "Heyyyy, how ya doing?!" and just started talking to everyone. They said, "I thought you said he was quiet" and I said, "I thought he was!"

My daddy walked me down the hallway and the foyer into the living room and handed me off to Bill. In the pictures, my father is behind me, stepping on the back of my gown as we were going in to have cake and punch. Everyone had asked or assumed that we were going to be leaving for our honeymoon in my car. We knew that our friends, who had never seen me in anything but jeans before, would be out to prank us. Bill had told them we were staying in our rented trailer. My orange Nova was a piece of junk, but we actually left in Bill's red truck. We also weren't in the trailer for them to harass us, since my Dad had given us money to go to San Antonio, Texas. We found out later that our friends went and rocked the trailer hooting and hollering, only to find out we were not there. Our friends spent time dressing up my junky old Nova only to watch us get in Bill's little red truck and drive off.

So we headed down to San Antonio which has a beautiful Riverwalk that is lighted at night. We went to see the Alamo, caves, and went to a local restaurant that was called the Magic Time Machine. It had different cubicles that were based on anything from a space capsule to Daniel Boone, and waiters and waitresses were dressed in costumes. Then we had a meal we never will forget; it was a Mexican dish. It was in the most beautiful restaurant that had a terrarium inside of it with all the plants. It was just gorgeous. The meal was just fabulous and the service from the wait staff was just phenomenal. We were going to spend the big bucks that night. The meal cost us five dollars and fifty cents each, but it was one of the best meals I think we had at that time.

A Lesson Learned

It amazed me that they had known each other, but it seemed that the timing of life was not right. The way we expect things to go is not usually the way they actually go.

Prayer

Holy Spirit, I ask you to lead and guide me into all truth, that you put the right people in my life and remove those in it that should not be there! I ask for your wisdom and your word to guide me!

CHAPTER 5

Story of My Birth

I WAS BORN IN Natchez, Mississippi on December 1, 1979. I was supposed to have been born mid-December, but I was actually born about two weeks early. This is how my mom and dad recall that day:

Robin:

November thirtieth was a beautiful day. I was cleaning out the chicken shed, and I had gone inside to clean the house and cook supper. Bill was supposed to have gone on a fishing trip to the Gulf of Mexico. He did some commercial fishing on the side for extra money. He had planned this for months. Mainly because you were not supposed to be born for a couple weeks and he was planning to go out of town that day. When he came home from work, I had started hurting and having pains: labor pains. They were getting pretty regular, but I wasn't in any tremendous amounts of pain. When he came home, I told him I thought I was in labor. He said,

"I knew you were gonna try to mess up my fishing trip".
I told him, "No, for real!"

So he kept loading up fishing gear the whole time. He didn't believe me, so he continued putting his fishing gear into his truck. I went and called my mama,

"Mama I think I'm in labor, but Bill doesn't believe me. Can I come up to your house?" Later he would tell me he walked by the open door and heard me and thought "for a joke, she's really carrying this a bit far." I didn't know that he was there and had overheard me talking to her. So that's when he said we should go down to Gene's house, one of our family friends. He thought that if it was false, him and Gene could leave from there, but if it was real, it would be closer to the hospital.

So we went up to Gene's house, and Billy, Gene's wife, started saying "for a joke, she's carrying this a bit far". When we got there, the pains were definitely becoming closer together and more severe, so we knew we better go ahead and go to the hospital. Bill was still in his coverall camo fishing gear and hunting clothes. After we had been admitted to the hospital room, Billy and I were in the room, and they come in and check me. They said,

"He's not going to be born until six in the morning tomorrow, so we said okay. Well it wasn't but twenty or thirty minutes later that I started having severe pains, so I grabbed Billy literally by the collar and told her,

"Get me some help! I'm having this baby now." And she was patting me like, telling me to calm down. I pointed down and said, "LOOK!" And she looked, and there you were coming. And I mean, they wheeled me FAST into the delivery room, and brought a bottle of laughing gas, which is what doctors gave you back then. They threw the bottle of laughing gas at me and they were like here, breathe. Meanwhile, they were trying to get my legs up in the stirrups, which they barely did before you were born, just a little bit after midnight. So I've often said that the way you were born is how you have been your whole life. You came early and not needing anything. Bill echoed: "In a hurry, yeah. Always in a hurry."

A Lesson Learned

Sometimes in life, you just have to trust your gut. In this case, quite literally, regardless of the opinions of even your closest relationships. There are many of mothers out there that have had Godly intuition and not realized it.

Prayer

Holy Spirit, I ask you to be led by you, to never be in a hurry, and to always be ready to listen to those around me!

CHAPTER 6

It Gets a Little More Complicated

Robin:

WHEN YOU WERE ONE month old, you got sick, so I took you to the doctor. He told me that you just had a cold or a virus, so he gave you some medicine. I was staying with mama because your dad finally went on that fishing trip that he wanted to go on. He had been down there before and made around eight hundred dollars or something because they caught eight hundred pounds or so of fish.

You were four weeks old, and I was giving you the medicine the doctor had told me to give you, but I noticed I would go in and change your diaper, but it wasn't wet. Then mama and I noticed you really weren't drinking that much. We thought maybe it was the medicine the doctor gave you or you were just not getting any sleep. So, I took off your socks and your little feet were ice cold and almost blue. I took off your diaper and your little penis was a blue-black color. It wasn't funny, but my mama asked what color Bill's penis was because she thought that maybe it was that color since he was Indian. I got up and called the hospital because something was not right. They said to get you there immediately– something was wrong. So mama and I grabbed you up and took you to the hospital. It was near the end of December, and I remember it was really cold so I had put a blanket over your face. I took you to the ER, and it was just full of people who had been there waiting, people with broken bones and other serious injuries. You could see all kinds of situations. But when the nurse pulled back the blanket and saw you, you were almost blue. It was a male nurse, and I still remember his name to this day. They would say, "Norman get in here, Norman get in here." And so Norman came in and it was like, "What do you want, can't you see how slammed I am?" And when he saw you he was like, "Oh, my gosh." And they grabbed you and took you up immediately to the pediatric intensive care.

They called the doctor in and within just a little bit, the doctor came out and told me that you were in heart failure. That you had an illness called pericarditis which is a virus that attacks the heart and the lining of the heart. And he said that yours had gotten so severe that you were in liver and kidney failure. That was why you weren't urinating; your liver had turned over, which is one of the first signs of death. Your heart was enlarged. After getting the diagnosis, the doctor came in and he told me that you would not live till the morning; they gave you three to eight hours to live. He asked me where my husband was and I told him that he was out of town fishing. Norman said that you need to get him here and I asked "Well, what can he do?" He said there's nothing he can do, you will need him for you. This baby will not live.

Bill:

We were fishing in Buras-Triumph, which is about as far south in the US that you can go. Gene and I were gar fishing around two in the morning, and we saw lights coming. We thought it was the game wardens checking on us, but we weren't doing anything illegal this time. They came up and the first thing he asked was,

"Is there a Gene or Bill Decker in here?" We were both really confused because we did so much crap in the past, but we were not doing anything this time. He then asked if either of us knew Billy D. Gene said that that was his wife. Then the warden said that Billy had called and said that Robin was at the hospital with my son, who apparently only had three to eight hours to live. The problem was, we were about six hours away.

When I got there, you were up on the third floor, so I took an elevator up to that floor. When I got off the elevator, I took a left; it was a really small hospital. I saw Robin sitting on the floor beside a water fountain, and back then I didn't believe in God. I figured some people needed a crutch to lean on in life. I didn't have any problems with people who did because I figured, some people need something to believe in. That was my opinion back then. So, when I got off the elevator and saw Robin sitting there on the floor crying, I had already gave you up as dead, so my thought was, how do I comfort her? What do I say to her? How do I say it? This was the only thing that was in my mind the whole drive back and even when I got off the elevator; she's sitting on the floor beside the water fountain crying! I thought oh God, what do I do? I figured I was too late.

Robin:

I was not in church at that time, but I had been raised as a child in church and my grandmother was a devout Christian. I knew about the Bible and God. But I wasn't living for God. I remembered the scripture that said; if two or more of you ask anything in my name, and you believe you will receive... and I thought I'm one and my mama is two. So, I went down to the lobby where they had a pay phone and called my grandmother, and she said she was in church. So I called the church and told them they needed to go get my grandmother. So they went and got her and I said, "Mama they said that Shawn is gonna die, and I need you to pray." Later I found out that she went back out and they stopped the church service immediately and the whole service stopped and started to pray.

These were holy ghosts filled, Pentecostal, believing, laying of hands, healing people. So she started praying, and I went from the lobby of the hospital back up to your pediatric intensive care unit. My mama was with me, and she said that she will never forget what the doctor said. The doctor came out of your room, shaking his head, while taking off his mask, saying I don't know what in the hell is going on, but he's coming back, he is coming back. And you were coming back too. The next morning they still didn't expect you to live, but you had made it to the next morning. In the meantime, I had to call the state troopers to find your daddy in the Gulf of Mexico to get him to come back.

My mama came after church, and she prayed again. You

had lived through the night, and they sent us to a hospital that was about two and half to three hours away in Jackson, Mississippi. It was a huge hospital but had a pediatric heart specialist that could examine you. A woman in the hospital actually walked up to us and put money into our pockets so that we would have enough gas money to take you to that hospital.

We found out that you had pericarditis and a heart murmur, and it was estimated that only one out of one hundred thousand babies were born with it at that time. Pericarditis currently accounts for less than twenty percent of the emergency visits of children without prior heart disease presenting with chest pain to a tertiary pediatric emergency setting. Even with adequate treatment, certain types of pericarditis has a mortality rate between forty and seventy-five percent. At the time I was informed that only one percent of them live, and of the one percent, one hundred percent are vegetables their whole life due to the extent of heart damage. They said you would never be able to be active. Your chest bones were inverted, and because of that, it limited your oxygen supply to your lungs, literally. It also limited how well your heart beat because it would hit against the chest wall. They also said you had an enlarged heart at that time so your chances to live were even less. They put you on a heart medicine to slow your heart rate down. We took you to another heart specialist, and he didn't really give us hope that you would live past your first year. I will never forget, we took you home and I saw a friend of mine. I told her what was going on, and she said,

"Here, I would like you to have this."

It was a glass angel. She said to put it by your bed so that you would always have an angel to watch over you. I took it home and I did, I put it at the foot of your bed. You weren't even supposed to live that first year. I will never forget that sometimes I was afraid of even getting attached to you. You would be sleeping and I would be afraid to even walk over to the crib because I wasn't sure if you were going to be alive. I remember sometimes I would get our next door neighbor, which was an older man, Mr. Al, to check and see if you were okay or even breathing.

Bill:

To help you understand my state of mind during all of this, I would never pick you up unless you had to be changed or something because I didn't want to become attached to you. I was still convinced you would die. I had no faith at the time, and didn't know anything about it. I was always a super light sleeper, especially after I got out of the service. We had put your crib right at the foot of our bed, so if you just breathed heavy or turned over, I would bolt up. I would see you laying there, and I would just watch for your chest to move. Sometimes I would pull the blanket back to where I could see if you were breathing. I don't know how many times I looked at you and thought you were dead. I would put my hand on you real gentle and you would still feel warm. Sometimes I would put my hand in front of your mouth if I couldn't see your breath. That first year was the hardest year of my life. Every day I would think, that's the end of it.

1980 – My Dad, Sister and I. You can notice how sick I appeared at that time.

A Lesson Learned

No matter how impossible the situation looks, no matter how close to death, God can make up the difference and God can help you through. He can give you courage when you have none and He can sustain you when you have no hope. He is the difference, He is your hope!

Prayer

God, I ask you in Jesus' Name to come into this situation and make the difference, to give me hope where there is none. I pray you would help me to know that no matter how bad it looks on the outside, you love me. This hard time is not your will and you have plans for my success and the success of my children. I pray that my life and my children's life will glorify you! I thank you in advance for all you're going to do in Jesus' Name!

CHAPTER 7

Moving to Idaho

Robin:

AFTER YEARS OF BEING estranged, Bill and his dad reconnected while I was pregnant. I had been writing Bill's Dad, and now Bill wanted to move back home. We bought a brand new Chevrolet truck, and I am telling you, they made the "lemon law" for that thing. We had eleven thousand miles on it when the head gasket blew going over the top of the lookout pass on the way to Idaho.

We moved to Idaho early May of 1980 when you were five months old. We remember the date because Mount Saint Hellen erupted about two weeks after we got there, and it was Mother's Day. I was amazed that there was snow on the flowers on Mother's Day that year. Being from Louisiana, I wasn't used to snow in May.

We hadn't been there more than a week or so when both Shawn and Nikki got sick. Then just a few days later your daddy and I also got sick. We were so sick that we literally would have to crawl on the floor to get over there to check on you two. We had rented us this lil' old apartment. His sister lived just up the street, at the end of the road. I was up visiting her one day with you, and I noticed this gray stuff falling from the sky, these little flakes. I was sitting there thinking, what is this, smog? Is this what they call smog? Grey stuff falling from the sky? But then it started piling up by the inches. I was with you in Pattie's house, and we turned on the radio to hear that Mount Saint Helen's, the volcano in Washington State, had erupted and blown. The plume of the ash and smoke was carried over into Idaho, about three hundred something miles. It was literally inches deep of ash. People who had respiratory problems or heart problems couldn't go outside.

1980 – My Mom and Sister – The Blue Chevrolet that was a Lemon in the background.

We were so concerned about you. We didn't want to take you out in all the dust because they said it was full of aluminum. So, we decided to stay with Pattie. Bill saw this old Italian guy on a tractor with a bucket scraping up ash. He asked him if he could have a job because he hadn't been able to get one. But when that ash hit, he got a job cleaning it up. It was supposed to be a temporary job, but he worked there right up until he got a job and went in the mines. He got the job with the City of Mullen making about six dollars per hour, cleaning up the ash. We had moved about seven times in two years. We had just moved from the apartment to a nice little house when you got sick again. That time it was pneumonia and they put you into the hospital. I wasn't able to find work because no one would keep you. They were too scared of your heart issues. So we only had the one income from Bill's job with the city.

Your daddy wanted to go fishing, but he literally did not have a coat. I remember I would pray, God he needs a coat, it's getting to be winter time. He really needs a coat. We don't have the money, but he needs a coat. So one day he went fishing and he came back with a brand new blue, goose down coat. Back in that day there was no warmer material than goose down. This coat was kinda balled up by a tree by the river/creek. He found it and shook it out, dusted it off and it fit perfectly. He came home and told me about how lucky he was to find it. I told him I've been praying for a coat for you. "Praying!", he said, "there is nothing to that praying stuff". Back then, you couldn't have convinced him of that stuff. He said praying had nothing to do with it, if I hadn't went fishing, I wouldn't have seen that coat. But I told him that God gave him that coat. And he argued, "No He didn't, I found that coat. Some fool lost it in the water!"

A Lesson Learned

God cares about the little things, even a coat! It just takes you asking him. Then after he does it, give him the credit and the glory for being involved in your life.

Prayer

Father, it says in your word that if I ask anything in your name and according to your will, You will do it. Father, I ask you for my need and am willing to follow you and do your will, and thank you for my need in Jesus' Name!

CHAPTER 8

Dominick–
The Old Italian

DOMINICK WAS THE OLD Italian that Bill met on the tractor. Dominick really turned out to be a saving angel for us. For the record, Dominick's mother's name was Mary, his father's name was Joseph, and he was born on the twenty-fifth of December. And he was, at that time, the only savior Bill and I ever knew. He offered for us to move into an old mine cabin that he oversaw. It was at the end of his property, which was about fifteen hundred acres. It was called the Beacon Light Silver Mine. This old mine cabin was half dilapidated. It was made of rough sawn two by twelve lumber planks. It was solid as dickens, but it didn't look like it was. It had a toilet but didn't have running water. You had to take a hose and run it into a bucket, fill it with water, then dump it by hand. The shower was an old rubber hose that was hung over into a galvanized tub.

Part of the two back bedrooms had floors that had literally

rotted to where there was ground there. So we took a wheel barrow and mixed cement in it and filled it to make floors. Bill put a concrete slab in there, raised it where the commode was, and put a tub in there. Our water came from a well. It was gravity fed to the one spigot in the house. It would take about three times as long as a typical toilet, but it was an improvement. At least now we didn't have to dump water into it anymore, and we could actually take a bath.

1981 –The exterior of the cabin we lived in.

With a little wood cook stove, we would heat the house and cook. So things were finally starting to look up!

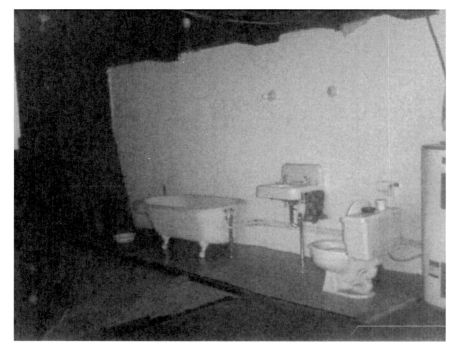

1981 –The interior of the cabin we lived in.

Now all of this was very foreign to me. Even though I had grown up on a farm and knew how to work, I never had to cook on a wood cook stove. But Bill, on the other hand, was right at home. My washing machine broke, so Bill got me an old timey kind, the kind with a ringer washing machine. That is the one with the two rollers that would squeeze the water out as your clothes ran through it. So on one occasion, I was running the clothes through it, and I got my hand caught in it. I literally ran my hand through it right up to my elbow. I did not know that there was a button that you could hit on top that would release it, so the only thing I knew to do was reverse it! So I ran my arm and hand back through it to back it out. When Bill came home that evening, I told him what I had done. By this time, my hand was black and blue. He couldn't believe that I didn't know that there was a little button, that if anything happens like that, you just take your fist and hit it and the jaws flop apart so you can get your hand out.

That particular year we were running behind getting the fire wood, so he would always split it for the winter ahead. But this year he was only able to get it cut, he hadn't been able to get it split. He had put it in the wood shed. There were about twenty-one cords of wood that he had cut. I was so proud of him. There was a job with this company called Red Path, a mining company that would sink the original mine shaft. They paid those guys good money, twice what he was making at the city. Your daddy, he would go down every day and sit on this guy's steps in the morning until he got there. He found out what time he arrived to work and got there an hour before he would. He would ask the guy if he was hiring. The guy would say, no not today. Daddy would say "Okay, well I'll see ya tomorrow." They told him they would call him if they were hiring and not to come back. But he did this every day for about two weeks. They got to where they would come in and just say, "Morning Bill," and go on in. After about two or three weeks, they asked him in and offered him a job.

Bill:

Yeah, one morning, one of the guys didn't show! So Clark left me with Gary which was one of the superintendents. So I started working with this guy named Gary Van Brooky. Gary asked me if I had run something like this before. I don't really remember what I told him, but I am sure I probably lied to him. Gary asked me if I knew how to use the equipment. They had a huge front end loader called an articulated Pettibone®. I was desperate for the job and I had used farm equipment in the past, so I lied and said yes. Gary climbed up in the articulated Pettibone® and showed me how to use it and where all the buttons were. He took me through one trip to show me the steps and how to fill the bucket. I frantically watched everything he was doing. Then he said okay, now you try it, and I did terrible. I had no idea how to get the bucket full, and I didn't know how to shift it. It was just all sorts of stuff I didn't know how to do. At first, I couldn't even get the bucket half full. I think Gary could tell I didn't know what I was doing. So he told me he would be back in a while. After a few hours, I had the hang of it.

Later, after we got to know each other, he asked me, "now tell me the truth, you didn't know how in the hell to run an articulated Pettibone®, did ya?" I said I didn't even know what articulated Pettibone® was! He said "I figured, well you're a quick study. I could see you were real nervous. I figured if I just left you alone, you would either make it or break it." I told Gary, I was just so desperate for a job. I just remember he had the bluest eyes I ever saw.

So I got the job running the loader, but then I got a promotion to what was called a top lander. A top lander rode a bucket that went down the elevator shaft into the ground where the ore would be loaded into this bucket and they would bring it back up the surface and dump it. What I actually did was make sure the bucket went down, they loaded it, and then it would come up. When it would pass me, I would grab it and step out on it and then it would go up probably about three stories. I would step off it, hit a button, and it would dump it out into that shoot. That was my job. I tended that bucket all day long. There was a little shack up there with a heater in it because Idaho gets really cold in the winter, sometimes even ten to twenty degrees below freezing.

Robin:

You were about two at this point, and we lived up there at Beacon Lake by then. Things had been kind of rough financially, but it was starting to look up with your Dad's new job as this top lander. He was making good money; about sixteen dollars per hour then which would be like fifty dollars per hour these days. It was January 1982, I got a phone call at the cabin, and they told me that your Daddy had been hurt in an accident and that I needed to get to the hospital. As I hung up the phone, I was kinda pacing the floors because I had Nikki who was six then, and I wasn't quite sure what to do.

I called up Bill's Brother-in-law who was usually in the bars drinking, but that night I told him that I needed him to go get his wife Patty. I let him know that Bill had been hurt and ask if she could come keep you kids. He brought Patty up to the Cabin and took me down to the hospital. When I got to the hospital, they had Bill in the E.R. and Gary Van Brooky was there. He sat with me while they were working on Daddy, but my mind was so frantic and stuff because they told me that it had been a serious injury and that he may lose his foot or part of his leg. This was about as severe of an injury as you could get. But Gary sat there with me, even though he was a total stranger to me. He would keep me talking about things the whole time. Looking back now, I realize that he was just trying to keep my mind off of the horrible news about what was going on in the other room with Bill as they were working on him.

The hospital was so small that they realized his injuries were out of their league. So in the middle of winter time in Idaho, they loaded him and me in the ambulance to take us to another hospital that was in Coeur D'Alen, Idaho, which was thirty-five miles away over a rough, icy, and bumpy road. They bound up his wounds and started just shooting anesthesia and stuff into his leg, trying to keep the pain down. Dr. Gesin was the surgeon at Coeur D'Alen Hospital that worked on him. He was the best Orthopedic surgeon they had there in that city. In Silverton Idaho, the Doctor said,

"Mr. Decker, in my opinion, you are probably going to lose your foot. But if anybody can save that foot, he's in Coeur D'Alen, and I'm gonna send you there."

They called what happened to him a partial amputation because it literally yanked his entire foot loose. It broke his ankle and pulled the entire pad off of his heel. The only thing that was holding his foot on was the four top tendons on the front of his foot. His leg had slipped off the side of the bucket he would ride and an eye bolt went into the side of his leg, just below his knee. It literally ripped the skin all the way down. It tore the whole calf muscle loose from his leg. They would pull the calf muscle and lay it to the side as they would shove the injections into his leg to start to numb the pain. It was so bad that they couldn't even stitch the calf muscle back together; they had to just let it heal from the inside out together. He was in the hospital for over two weeks the first time.

When he finally got to come home, he had to stay in the bed for almost a month; he couldn't even get out of bed. Then he moved to a wheelchair which he could kinda start to get around in. He was ready to be able to move around but was so weak that just peeling potatoes would wear him out. Then he had to go back into the hospital for two more weeks to do a skin graft on his foot because there was no skin even there. They took the skin off of his thigh in about two inch squares.

During this same time period, it was a severely hard winter. Bill was hurt and Shawn got pneumonia and had to be put in the hospital. I took you in to the Doctor and I said

"Doctor, before you touch my baby, you need to know that I don't have any money or insurance."

He said, "I don't care. Your baby is still entitled to the finest medical care available. Take him to the hospital and I'll be right there." As I was leaving with you, the ladies at the front register started pounding on the desk saying I needed to pay. I looked back towards him helplessly, and he came up and patted me. He said,

"Honey it's okay, just take the baby to the hospital". I turned at the door to look back, and I heard him just ringing them out, "don't you ever stop my patients over money".

I took you to the hospital thinking you might have heart failure again, but you had pneumonia instead. When your Daddy was hurt, that was the fourth time that you had had the pneumonia. Shawn was in one town thirty-five miles away in a hospital and Bill was thirty-five miles away in a different hospital. I stopped by there to see you (Shawn) one morning on my way to go see Bill. When I came back to check on you, you were not there! You were not in your room where you were supposed to be, so I started freaking out because I thought my baby was gone. A mom's mind will just panic, thinking of reasons why their baby is not anywhere on the hospital floor. The nurses started looking at each other really funny and confused. I was like, where is my baby? It turns out, you had climbed out of the baby bed in the hospital area and went down and found Bill's sister, who was also in the hospital, and you were up in the bed with her.

Bill had come home from his skin graft. That year we got thirty-five feet of snow right above us. Since he did not have the chance to split the wood and now had been hurt, I had to split all the wood for the wood stoves that had only been sawed up. I was out playing with you kids in the snow and your Daddy was on crutches watching us. Me and you kids had been sledding down the mountain on one of those round saucers. As I went down the hill, the sled turned around and I began going down backwards. I reached out and put my hand out to stop the sled. Well, I wasn't familiar with how hard snow was, and it just snapped my wrist back. I got off the sled, and I was nauseous. I told everybody I think I broke my wrist and they were like no, if you broke it you'd know you broke it. I told them I didn't know if I broke it, but I think I broke it. So they said to wiggle my fingers, bend my wrist, and all that other stuff. So, I just packed snow and put ice bags on it. I went on chopping wood and feeding the animals. I would have to throw fifty-pound bags of feed on my shoulder and snow shoe about one hundred fifty yards.

About three days later, my arm started turning yellow-green. This was an indicator that marrow may be leaking out. So I went to the doctor that day with Nikki and Bill, who was still on crutches. I got to the doctor, and he asked me when I did it. I said I had about three days ago. He said,

"Honey, all I can say is you are one gritty little girl because this thing is broken." You fractured it length wise not sideways. So he put it in a cast. I went home, but I had to continue to split wood, shovel snow, and take care of animals. Dominick's oldest son, Steve, would come up and help me with some of it when he could.

One morning, I heard the dog barking during the day, and I looked out through the snow and saw a man just staggering. So I yelled, "who are you" and I don't know if he couldn't hear me or what, but he didn't answer me. He kept staggering, and I was getting a little scared since I was alone so far from everyone. Our nearest neighbor was a half mile down the mountain. I went and grabbed the shotgun, came out on the porch, and put a shell in the chamber. When he heard the shell, he started yelling, "Robin, don't shoot. It's Ron!"

He was the snowplow guy. The snow was so bad that year that the snow plow got stuck and he had to walk up there to call for help. That was the winter after your Dad was hurt. The snow had come almost to the top of the chicken house building. Bill would sit in the window in his wheelchair watching me. All he could see was the tip of the shovel come up and snow fly over the bank I had made. The bank would get so high, sometimes it would just go back in the path I was trying to make. All I was trying to do was keep a path shoveled out to all the chickens so they didn't die.

That year it was really bad, and I didn't really know the Lord. We laugh about it now because when we would hang out with our friends, we would smoke pot, drink, then read Revelations stoned out of our mind. It was scary! But I knew that there was a God. There is a country song that goes, "Lord

I hope this day is good." I remember I would talk to God, but I really didn't know him, and I didn't know he was a good God. But I do remember different instances where I would pray and Bill would be almost cussing, "there's no God to hear you". And I would be like well, you just be quiet so he can hear me. The following year got harder because he wasn't working. The company started trying to fight his workers compensation because he could not go back to work a year later.

Bill:

I remember starting to get really concerned about the money, but Doctor Gesin wouldn't release me. Finally, I kept at it to where he said,

"Look, you go try it and see how it goes with you, but if you can't handle it, don't force yourself to do it. I'll deal with the workers compensation." So I went up to the Red Path, and they were willing to let me do half days and I'd work just in the dry. I cleaned lights and recharged their miner's batteries and that sort of stuff. I didn't do that too long, that foot would swell up so much at night that I would almost have to cut my pants off. So I didn't do that long.

Robin:

So, our good fortune of the good job, that money, it ended really shortly after him getting hurt. That following Christmas was a desperate one. There was literally no money. My parents had given me this gold necklace when they had money. I pawned it for about sixty dollars, so it was nice for the time. I was able to buy Bill a guitar at a pawn shop, and you and Nikki one present a piece. We had a Christmas tree that year because I went and cut it from a national forest.

Bill had gotten the tree every other year, but he couldn't get out there to do it this year. It was so bad that I climbed up a pine tree with my saw. I was getting ready to saw it, but then I dropped my saw. I had to climb back down the tree, climb back up the tree, and I cut it out. When I got back down to the ground, it was rotten. The top of it was so rotten that I had to climb up another tree and cut the top out of it. The snow was so deep that you couldn't see the little trees. So you'd find a bigger one that had a nice top and go up and cut the top out of it. I did that and we had us a tree. That was the first year, by the second year things had gotten even worse financially. I didn't even have anything to sell.

Our friends back then would smoke pot, drink, and they would bring up pot and booze almost every visit. People would bring up marijuana, beer, wine, whiskey, and all that other stuff. I remember thinking; I wish somebody would bring a package of hamburgers. We didn't go hungry, but we just ate beans, and ate beans, and rice and beans, and more rice, and homemade bread and beans.

God bless Dominick, because he could see me getting so discouraged at times. I think he admired my hard work and grit. He would come up and he would tell me with an Italian accent,

"Robby," he said, "the man in the white house, he don't sleep no better than you do at night. He's sleepin' no better than you do in that cast-iron bed. He don't get no cleaner, no cleaner than you, in a marble shower than you do in your nice bear claw tub. And Robby, your belly is no fuller on beans and bread then if ya had a ribeye steak."

He would teach me lessons like that about life. I was really anemic back then so he would bring up bottles of wine because he said it was good for my blood to drink. Dominick would always make Robin drink a little cup of wine. Then he'd tell Bill, "you damn Indian; you stay out of her wine." But Dominick always kept Bill in beer so that he didn't need to drink any of the wine anyway. Plus, at that time, Bill didn't especially like wine!

A Lesson Learned

There are just certain people in this life that I know God has put there. Many people have called them an angel and a saving grace. But regardless, I believe that God knew that person would play a part in changing your destiny. These people show you that, even in the worst time, he is there. I also believe that the devil tries to put people in your life, but they are not there to help you but to get you off track.

Prayer

God, I ask that you send the right people in my life, and give me the wisdom and grace to see the right ones from the wrong ones. I also ask that I would be the right person in other people's lives. I ask that I would show them your grace and mercy that you have shown me, to be kind and give hope.

CHAPTER 9

Here Come the Cops

Robin:

IT WAS REALLY TIGHT, and your daddy still couldn't go to work. This one lady I knew had let me come down and waitress on the weekends. I would make some money, but it was still hard because daddy wasn't getting much money from workers compensation then. I never will forget that Christmas Eve. We didn't have anything for Christmas dinner, no presents, nothing. I stared out of the window, and my heart stopped. I was still kinda praying, and up came a cop car over the hill. Bill said he started praying too, but it was not for the same reason– it was because we had pot in the house.

I thought to myself, no, that's not what I was asking for, but then I turned and told Bill to hide the pot. He was on the couch and was starting to get to where he could get up and get around some, but he couldn't move quickly or anything. I'm like Bill, hide the pot there's a cop. Nobody came up to where we lived at, especially in the winter. We were at the end of the road, at the top of a hill, where there was tons of snow.

This cop came up, and he said that they were from "policemen's benevolent fund." He said someone had given them our name because we were having a hard year. He had a couple of boxes, and in them was everything for a Christmas dinner. Fresh milk, oranges, apples; you don't think much of that stuff these days, but boy back then, it was something. There was the turkey, dressing, cranberry sauce, milk, and even cookies. For y'all kids, (Shawn and Nikki), little socks, mittens, and a cap. There was a little toy in there which was exciting because we literally didn't have a toy in the house. That was the first year Bill gave me a box of chocolate covered cherries for fifty cents a box. That was our Christmas. That was all that he could give me that year, but to me that was huge. We always enjoyed Christmas.

1983 –The Christmas gifts from the Policemen.

Bill had made Nikki a doll house. He'd sit back in my little chair and take the big butcher knife and cut out cedar shingles. He didn't have any power tools except maybe a power drill. He had handsaws and stuff; he used them to make you kids little Lincoln Logs® type blocks. Ever since then, I have had a soft spot for the policemen's benevolent fund. Even years later, if I can afford to give to them, I always do. I always remember what they did for us that year.

A Lesson Learned

There are so many programs and resources out there in today's society. Don't be prideful and not willing to use any of them, but also never abuse the system because there are people out there that really need it.

Prayer

Give me the wisdom to look around and to see those around me. Those that I meet and run into, to be a help to others around me, and to realize how much less others have then me! Give me the grace and wisdom to look further than just my walls!

CHAPTER 10

Here Come the Bills

Robin:

THE HOSPITAL BILLS WERE still coming in from you, and your dad's medical care. You were like two or three years old then. You had been to over ten different doctors and hospitals. When we left Idaho, we owed fourteen different doctors and hospitals; it was over thirty-seven thousand dollars after paying on it for a year.

There were several different miracles in that time frame. We would send all these different doctors and hospitals, five dollars each a month. I had to do hand written letters. I would say,

"To whom it may concern, I know I owe you this large sum of money, but all I can pay you is five dollars right now. When I get more, I will pay you."

If we had any extra, we would give it to the one we owed less on so we could take his five dollars and give it to another one we owed more to. A hospital called to say they were going to turn our account over to a collection agency because I wasn't paying enough. I told them we were paying twelve or fourteen of them and working minimum wage jobs. I said that whenever I made more I would give it to them and that when I paid another off, they would get their five dollars. We had been paying your doctor that was in Natchez, Mississippi faithfully for a year or two, a little every month. One day I got a letter from him saying,

"The bill is considered to be paid in full per Dr. Jordanson's instructions. Have a Merry Christmas." Praise God!

He just wrote off our remaining balance, about sixty dollars. That gave us five dollars more to put on somebody else.

Then there was when you had pneumonia in Coeur D'Alen, and I told that doctor that I didn't have any money. They told me to go talk to the financial aid people and tell them that there was a law called the Halliburton obligation. We owed thousands to that hospital, but it received federal funding due to that law. They had to tear your hospital bill up right there.

A Lesson Learned

I know now that a lot of these things were not God's will, but due to not knowing how to hear his voice, what his promises are, and different ways to come out of these problems, we spent much longer in some of these situations than we had to. Even still, I have learned that if you will be diligent and faithful, God will always help you to come out of every situation, no matter how impossible it may seem.

Prayer

God, give me the courage to confront this situation and stay in hope when there seems to be no hope. Help me to be diligent and know that you will give me your favor to come out of this situation at record speeds, in Jesus Name, Amen!

CHAPTER 11

Shawn's First Memories

ABOUT SIX MONTHS LATER, we moved to Mulan, Idaho where we would remain for the next five years. My step grandfather lived in a little mobile home, which was more like a camper. I still have a few personal memories of him from when I was four years old. He was a tall, thin man with white hair. I remember he let me sit on his old wooden fence. There are very few photos of me before the age of four, one because we were so poor, but also because I was never supposed to have lived that long. My parents told me that they did not want all the additional memories. My dad told me that it would take him several years after I turned the age of two to really begin to have a bond with me because he had never expected for me to make it. I have very few pictures of me before the age of six. But one of the prized pictures is of me was when I was about four years old. One of the girls was down working near the mine and had a camera. So she took this picture and gave it to my parents:

1984 –Shawn E. Decker - The prized photo of me, taken by the lady working at the mines.

I was about four years old, and this was just the beginning of me trying to be a pyromaniac (or just a maniac, depending on who you ask), which would last for the next twenty years. I had an absolute fascination with pressing everything to the limits. In part, I think this was due to the health problems that I had when I was small. I would black out every time that I would get a spanking or get overly excited. If my mom or dad decided to spank me, which would later happen very often, I would black out. Since they were bothered more by the blackouts than by some of the behavior, they would do their best to not spank me.

I was starting to get completely out of hand by the time I was four, so my mom had taken me to the doctor to see if there was anything they could do. The doctor had asked my mother what would happen when I was being spanked. She explained that I would go limp, my eyes would roll back into my head, and I would pass out. I was pretty unruly at the time so as they were speaking, I was messing with the stuff in the doctor's office that I was not supposed to be. She had told me to stop several times. The doctor asked for her to demonstrate what happened when I was spanked. So she popped me in front of the doctor and out I went. The doctor checked me out and said that my vitals were okay. My mother's concern was whether or not it was causing long-term damage. The doctor did not believe there would be any damage so he told my mother to spank me when I misbehaved, and if I passed out, to spank me when I woke up.

This would be the beginning of many of the spankings I would have in my life. After one of the spankings, I had asked my mom why she did it. She said she only did it when I was bad. So, I made a confused motion with my hands and said, "but I am bad all the time". This is a memory that has stuck with me to this day. The cycle of spanking, blacking out, and resuming spanking would continue for the next several years. One of the much needed spankings came right around this time frame.

I was about four years old, and I loved fire. My mother had one of the old white covers with the white southern style fringes on the bottom. Well, everyone knows that cotton is very flammable, everyone but a four year old. I was a one hundred percent country boy, and I was taking some matches and lighting the fringes of the bedspread on fire. I still remember how I enjoyed watching them light on fire, and most of them would go out immediately. The rest I would instantly blow out. Right as my mom walked into the room to find me lighting matches on those fringes, I looked back at my mom and didn't blow out the other ones. So, about five seconds later, half of the bed was on fire. She didn't know what to do; so she took the blanket and rolled it up in her hands and arms, making a circle, to cause the blanket to make a complete ball. But this hot, melting ball of cotton, rolled up on my mother's hands and arms and caused several burns. None of the burns were extremely severe, but they did cause her a lot of pain.

A Lesson Learned

It is a miracle that we even make it through this life at all many times. That our children make it through life, school, the doctors, or the surgeries; just that we make it one more day, it is God's Grace!

Prayer

Jesus, thank you for all that you have done for me and I ask you to give me grace and mercy for one more day. I ask you for protection over me and my house, teach us and guide us, so that we can avoid the pitfalls that so easily try to ensnare us. I thank you for your grace, and I ask for your wisdom. I know I have what I ask according to your word!

CHAPTER 12

Moving to Savannah

I WAS ABOUT FIVE, almost six years old and Dad was getting to where he could work pretty consistently. However, the market was so depressed up in that area of Idaho that my family was not really able to make it. We packed everything up and headed down to Savannah, Georgia. My dad had a 1984 Toyota pickup and it was this light tan color. He packed that thing up to the rim and then some, and off we go for a road trip. Driving from Mullen Idaho to Savannah Georgia, was a two thousand five hundred and twenty-one mile trip. Today, that trip would take about one day and thirteen hours. Back then, it took us three days. My dad was a country boy, and I remember we were heading through Phoenix, Arizona and he told me to shut up, sit down, and not say a word while he was driving. Being from the Rocky Mountains where it is one lane roads on switch backs, traffic and the six lane roads were a drastic change for him. All I remember is how nervous he was. When we would go through the big cities, I would lay on my seatbelt and go to sleep, but he would try to get me to read signs to keep me entertained.

Finally, we arrived in Savannah, Georgia. We arrived at my Aunt's house where we would spend the next few weeks while my dad got a job and a place for us to stay. Some of the family would watch me, but even at this time it was limited because of my medical problems and unruly behavior. Dad would tell me,

"Boy, you could tear up a steel ball bearing". This was funny to me because I actually figured out a way to do that later. I put it on a railroad track. It made them as flat as a pancake.

My aunt was a tall woman, and I could tell that she believed in God. You could tell this by how she acted. She was strict but nice and had a soft demeanor about her. I am pretty sure that I was slightly terrified of her.

My dad started working for his brother Butch almost immediately until he could find another job. My uncle was a big man and had served in combat during the Vietnam War. It was always funny to me how joyous of a man he was. He always reminded me of Santa Claus. Big, round, and loved to laugh. He always seemed to have more money than us, or at least spent it a lot different than how our family seemed to spend it. He would bring gifts every year for Christmas and birthdays. I used to think that it was impossible to make the man mad. Except one time when a man insulted his wife; he had been playing with a golf ball in his hand. He got so mad that he squeezed the golf ball and broke it. I later would try to break one, and I am telling you, that is a feat.

My uncle had two boys, one four years old and the other five years older than me. That made them about one year older than my sister. I never seemed to have much in common with them, maybe because I was so much smaller and younger than them. Karen was Butch's wife. She seemed to be a real Southern belle. Always prim and proper and, to this day, I don't think I have ever heard her yell. But I have heard stories that she can have a temper, but I have never seen it, and I don't really want to either. Butch is a big man, huge heart, bigger prankster and flirt, but you would have never met anyone better. One day we were at a restaurant and one of the little waitresses was sitting on Butch's lap. Someone asked Karen if it bothered her. She said,

"No, if he does anything, I'll choke him in his sleep". Butch heard her and laughed. But I am pretty sure everyone knew she was serious.

While dad was waiting for my mom to be able to come down to Savannah, he said that he would get bored at night and loved to read. All that he had to read was an old Jehovah Witness Bible. As he was reading the bible, he read a passage out of Leviticus 21:18- 20 NLV,

> [18] *No one who has a defect qualifies, whether he is blind, lame, disfigured, deformed, [19] or has a broken foot or arm, [20] or is hunchbacked or dwarfed, or has a defective eye, or skin sores or scabs, or damaged testicles.*

He told me that all he could think about for weeks was that scripture. He would wonder, what kind of God would not accept someone with a lame limb, or a droopy eye; he had a droopy eye since he was a child. This was a recurring thought he kept having, causing him to want to learn more.

Mom came down, and we found a place to move into. We stayed there for about a year until we moved out to Mr. Jackson's, which I will talk about a little later. She got a job at *House of Lee*. It was a family owned Chinese Restaurant. This was a waitressing job as my mom did not really have any formal education. But one thing about the family that owned the restaurant, they treated us like we were family. My mom would work here for the next four to five years. But just after a few months of her working, Pastor Larry came into the restaurant to eat and invited her to church. Dad had already decided that he was going to learn about "some of this God stuff," so he was trying a different church every week. My dad had heard about an End Times teaching that an Evangelist was going to do and really wanted to go to that. My mom wanted him to go to church with Pastor Larry at DeRenne Avenue Church of God. Dad didn't want to go and decided he was going to the End Times teaching that had interested him.

They head to the teaching, but they can't find where it is being held. So before it got too late in the evening, they decided to go ahead and go over to DeRenne Avenue. My dad said that the whole time he was there, he kept looking up at the ceiling wondering how much the wood beams must have cost. He thought they should have spent that money feeding the poor or something. But that next Sunday they went back and he got saved. The same man that thought God was just a crutch that people used because they needed something to believe in was saved. This had such an impact that my uncle Butch and his family, my uncle Benny (mother's brother), and all of us children started going to that church, just so they could see why my dad got saved.

Right around this time, my dad got a job at GB Cabinet Company. He would spend the next several years there doing every kind of side job there is, trying to make some extra money. He did a lot of call back work (correcting other people's mistakes), and spent a lot of his time alone. During this time, he really got turned on to some word-of-faith teaching. He would listen and re-listen to everything he had. From my perspective, all that seemed to be happening was him getting stricter and more legalistic. During the summers when something would happen and they didn't have someone to watch me, he would make me come to work with him. I would be his little gopher, running around fetching him tools and trying to stay occupied so I didn't get in trouble for being in something I wasn't supposed to be in.

A Lesson Learned

Religion is a horrible thing, and there are many of Pastors, Churches, Congregations and Christians that do not always accurately present the true nature of how Christ really is! So, instead, we should judge Christ for his actions, his example, and his demonstration of his love for us, and not judge Christ for something his followers have said or done.

Prayer

Lord, teach me your ways, the way you love me. Show me how to be more like you, so that others also see the God I know you can be in Me!

CHAPTER 13

Saved but Not Sanctified

DE RENEE AVENUE CHURCH OF GOD, is where we started going pretty much every Sunday. It wasn't too much longer after that I was saved by my Sunday school teacher, Mrs. Irma, when I was six years old. Because of this and many other things that she would do, she played a pivotal part in my life. She said that having a child-like Christian faith would forever be a part of my expectation of the goodness and graciousness of God. Much of it I would not really learn and realize for several years, but she instilled the concept of the simplicity of Christ that I think is sometimes missed today. Her husband's name was Milton, and he would do voices for puppet skits that they would do all the time. He was recently featured on The Voice and several other talent shows in the year two-thousand seventeen. I remember so many of the different bible stories because of him and Irma. They did such a wonderful job of keeping the bible fun and exciting for us.

From the time that I was about six to eleven, we lived in

a location which I remember as "Mr. Jackson's." He was the man that rented us an old, broke-down trailer. It would rain so much there that the septic tank would fill up with water and start to back up into the house. I remember having to deal with the smell and stench several times. My dad had a shop off to the left side of the trailer.

Well, I was a country boy living out at Mr. Jackson's. There were about five acres of grass lands right beside our home that were completely overgrown. All the kids in the neighborhood would spend time playing over in that section of grass. We would play Cops and Robbers, Hide and Seek, and any other game that we could make up. Beside that area was another five acres of woods that had large vines hanging down. It was our dreamland; we would pretend to be Tarzan, build forts to defend the world, etc. We would also play war, steal material from my dad's wood shop to build forts, make weapons, swing from the vines, and pretend we were in a different world. I would run though the grass fields, the overgrown ones that were covered with briars. Tough little young country boys become very accustomed to the pain of little scratches. I would run through them as fast as I could, not willing to slow down because we were usually playing war or tag. We would dive and hide in the grass and lie on the ground to not get spotted. Meanwhile, I was getting bit by red ants.

As discussed in earlier sections, I spent much of my early childhood very sick and being in and out of the doctors. I was the child that you see in the department store, underneath all the racks, having to touch everything. My mom started to notice that she would tell me to stop and I would ignore her. Even though this was not something that was necessarily atypical, it was becoming increasingly more annoying to my mom. She would tell me to stop doing things and I would not quit. She would ask if I heard her and I would tell her that I didn't. She started to notice this as a pattern after several days or about a week. I had ear infections before, so she asked me if my ears hurt and I told her no. This went on for a while, maybe a week or two. I believe I was about eight years old at this time, and by then my mom did not really check on me with showers and cleaning myself. One morning after about a week, I informed my mom that my ears were really hurting and that I wanted to go to the doctor. She called immediately and had an appointment set up for that very same day. Several hours later, we were at our appointment for the doctors to check out my ears.

The doctor did his typical checkup. After all of that, he checked my ear and realized I had a very bad ear infection. He said that if I had not come in then, I may have had permanent damage to my ear. Then he told me to take off my shirt. So, I took my shirt off, and my back and sides looked like someone had beaten me with a cat o' nine tails (a weapon for torture). I had scratches from my ankles all the way up to my neck. Some of scratches from the briars I had been running through had been pretty deep. He asked my mom to step out of the room and began to question me,

"Did your parents do this? How did you get these scratches? How long have you had this ear infection? When did you tell your mom about it? Are you sure today is the first time you brought it up to her?" The doctor then called my mother in the room to begin barraging her with questions too. Of course, there was no fault of my mom. The scratches where due to having a son that had an extreme tolerance for pain and was not willing to go to the doctor unless it was completely necessary. In this case, it was completely necessary. Once again, such a major issue was averted because of the perfect coincidental timing, or was it coincidental?

A Lesson Learned

God is your defender. When you do everything you know to do, know that God is your defender. Make sure you don't jump to assumption like this doctor did; you might not know the whole story.

Prayer

I ask you for patience to believe the best in people, to watch for the hurting and the lost, but to never be judgmental. Give me the wisdom to know the difference. I thank you for coming along my side and being my ever constant defender, Amen!

CHAPTER 14

More Fires

AS PREVIOUSLY TALKED ABOUT, I would have black outs if I would get too excited. However, this has not happened in several years. Once again, my fascination with fire got me in trouble. I would take matches or lighters, my mom was a smoker at the time so they were readily available, and go underneath my father's wood working shop and burn stuff. There was a lot of dry grass and wood around. My dad saw me doing this, and he knew what could happen, so he wanted to shock me, scare me, and discipline me. He sneaked up, grabbed me, and pulled me from underneath the shop. With one swing, he spanked me on my butt relatively hard. He said that I instantly went limp and blacked out. I still didn't learn to stop playing with fire, I just learned not to play with it under his shop.

A Lesson Learned

The patience of parents and God! Sometimes it is just as important to stop your kids from doing things as it is to teach them proper ways they can do them. Because a pyrotechnician gets paid, just saying! I heard a sermon with an illustration about fire one day. The statement I loved so much was, "a fire in the fireplace will keep your house warm, but a fire in the middle of the living room will burn your house down." The fire is not bad, but passion in the wrong place can destroy your life.

Prayer

Teach me, God, the difference between things being wrong in my life and things being in the wrong place. Show me if there are things that are good (sex, money, love, shopping), but teach me to keep them in proper places so that it keeps me and others safe and warm.

CHAPTER 15

The "Too Much" Garden

MY DAD, HAVING LIVED in Northern Idaho for so many years prior, had not been able to raise much of a garden like he had years before. He had never been able to raise squash or other summer plants because the climate did not allow for it. So, he decided to plant a garden that year that had about twenty mounds of five plant hills of cucumbers, yellow squash, zucchini squash, patty pan squash, tomatoes, and cherry tomatoes. That year, my dad would have my sister and I go and pick one to two five gallon buckets of just cucumbers every day. Not including the squash, zucchini, patty pan squash, and tomatoes, we would pick buckets of these every day. We were able to feed half of our neighborhood with the amount of vegetables we had come out of that garden that year. My parents were always givers, but that year, I remember particularly well. We gave so much away, people would almost be closing their doors when they would see us coming.

Over the next several years, we saw some of the returns on

the graciousness of God when it came to food when money was tight. Much of my childhood, all we could spend on the grocery bills was about sixty dollars a week. This was not much, considering many of the other people that I knew were spending about two to three times that every week. One thing I could say throughout my life is, me and my household have never seen a shortage of food. I believe that a big part of this was due to the my father's graciousness when it came to food. I learned to be a similar way by watching this example. I have learned that everyone is family. We may not have had much, but if we had extra, other people were welcome to it.

A Lesson Learned

I have seen too many pretentious people in my life that try to act like they are somewhere in life they are not. My family didn't have much, but what we had, others were welcome to. We didn't always have a garden with extra vegetables, but when we did, we shared. God has always richly blessed us with other people in our lives that also had similar hearts!

Prayer

Let me recognize the extra blessings in my life right now. Let me look around and see how I can bless those around me with my extra time, money, food, knowledge, contacts, etc. Teach me to not act like I am somewhere in life that I am not and help me to be willing to extend a hand! I thank you for your blessing and provision, in Jesus' Name, Amen!

Bell's Palsy

WHEN I WAS ABOUT EIGHT years old, I got Bell's palsy. To those who are not familiar with what Bell's palsy is, it is the paralysis of the face and sometimes the body. It usually subsides after three to twelve months. It can be caused by stress, inflammations, poor diet, etc. The exact reason as to why people get it are unknown, but it is speculated to be genetic (Wiki). According to Wikipedia, "About one and a half percent of people are affected at some point in their life. It most commonly occurs in people between ages fifteen and sixty. Males and females are affected equally." (Communities, 2000) "Bell's palsy affects about forty thousand people in the United States every year. It affects approximately one person in sixty-five during a lifetime. Worldwide statistics indicate a frequency of about two percent of the population."

This means that to have it before the age of fifteen is rare. When I got it, I just kind of woke up with it. I wasn't really expecting it or feeling funny. After a day or so I was unable to move the left side of my face, and my left hand was slightly affected as well. I remember that after I got it everyone kept asking me if I was okay. I remember how people treated me different, like I was retarded, having a mental illness or just stupid. My mom asked me how I was taking it; I told her I thought it was great. I could make all these horrible faces and people would laugh at me and feel bad for me. I was getting all of the attention and people would give me stuff and let me have my way. I was really enjoying it. I remember having to learn how to open a milk carton because my left hand would not want to move as well as the other. I had to learn to tilt my head so that when I drank milk out of the milk carton, it would not run out of my mouth.

I never remember being concerned about how I looked because of it. I just remember the difficultly that was involved with the nerves not wanting to function properly. This went on for about six to eight months. Then it went away on its own. However, the muscles in the left side of my face were slightly affected for many years to follow, slightly drooping. Even to this day some people say they can see it when I talk. But once again, the grace of God allowed me to walk away from that situation unscathed.

My mom took a job at Ryan's Steakhouse which was one of the few companies at the time that would even offer insurance to wait staff or cooks. This was especially rare because of all the health problems that my sister, whom was considered legally blind, and my dad with all his foot problems, and all the health problems I previously had. She would work here for the next seventeen years, twelve of them would be as a waitress and the last five as a manager when we kids were no longer home. This place would become almost home, a family away from home. To this day I am still friends with many of those people.

Many times I would go in with my mom to work and it would be several hours that we would have to kill before my dad could come get us. So I would vacuum some of the floors, roll silverware, or many other little tasks that the waiters/waitresses would pay me to do so they could go home early. My mom was one of the floor team leaders, and she would have to inspect their stuff before they could go home and man, she was tough. There were many times she would make us redo things.

A Lesson Learned

Many times in life, people accept disabilities as a way of life. They do this because they enjoy the attention, the pity, and the help. The problem is, they give up their faith in God for things to change. They fall in love with the sympathy given to them by people. However, I have noticed that most people with true disabilities are doing their best to be independent. For many people, it is nothing more than a mindset, because if you would take action, many disabilities would stop being one.

Prayer

(Non-Disabled) Let me be sensitive to the needs of those that truly need help. Let me never assume someone wants my help that does not really want it.

(Disabled) Father God, I ask You to show me if I look for sympathy from others. I ask for a new vision of what it looks like to be whole and healed and in you. I ask you to make the vision bigger in me than anything that is wrong with my body! Heal my soul and I will expect for my body to change in Jesus' Name!

CHAPTER 17

Pushing the Limits

WHEN I WAS TWELVE years old, I was such a dare devil. I always insisted on pushing the limits with everything I did. One day my friend Taetar and I were having fun around a big drainage ditch beside my cousin's house, which was just a couple of blocks from where we were at Mr. Jackson's (Trailer Park). When it rains in Georgia, it rains. Many times we would get two to four inches in one day, but it averaged about fifty-five inches a year, I believe. Around that area there were all these different kinds of drainage ditches that would allow the runoff rain to stop the area from flooding. We kids believed in playing in them. This was probably not the most sanitary thing to do in the afternoon, but we had a blast.

As it is many times in Georgia, it was ridiculously hot. Temperatures at that time were eighty-five to one hundred and nine degrees top. Many summer days were ninety-two to one hundred while the humidity felt like it was three thousand percent. We were all relatively poor and did not live in a community with public pools, but staying cool was a top priority. So in an attempt to stay cool, we would play in drainage ditches as much as possible. The fact that we did not die from some bad runoff or bacteria is a miracle in and of itself. But one day my friend and I were playing this game to see if we could jump across a ditch that was about six feet wide and about six to eight feet deep. We would take turns trying to jump this ditch. One would go and we might land in the bottom, then another would go and would almost make it. I was a very good jumper at the time. So, I got my running start and made the leap, and as I landed on the other side, my feet hit the side, and I slipped. I leaned forward as I did and fell face forward into a root that was sticking out from a tree that was right above the ditch. I hit it with my nose, pushing my nose upward, and I instantly knew that I had broken my nose. My nose was pouring blood, not that this was a shock, but I was in much more pain than what was typical. I was almost blacking out from the pain, and I was dizzy. My friend helped me back to my house.

My mom had not left for work yet that day, and she had to call off in order to take me to the doctor. Taking me to the doctor was always an issue since I never remember us having the money or insurance to cover the visits. I remember many of times we simply did not go to the doctor because that may be part of the grocery bill for the family that week. So if you went to the doctor, you made sure that it was for a good reason (like you were going to die). So we proceeded to the doctor that day.

On our way to the doctor, my face began to swell. By the time we reached the doctor, both eyes had swollen shut. My nose looked completely flat with no shape, and it was beginning to blacken. I had no ability to breathe through my nose at all. We arrived at the doctors and my mother filled out the appropriate paperwork. The doctor took me to get x-rays and discovered that I had, in fact, broken my nose. The break was so bad that I had actually broke it in three different places. I had a vertical center break, a horizontal center break, and then I had broken it in a circular pattern at the top of my nose at the edge of my brow. The doctors informed my parents that they needed to do emergency surgery. This surgery was going to be fifteen hundred dollars down payment, just for them to consider doing the surgery. Just going to the doctors at that time was us deciding not to buy groceries, so obtaining fifteen hundred dollars would have to be a miracle. My parents told the doctors that they would have to try and call some friends or the bank to somehow get the fifteen hundred dollars because they just did not have it at the moment. It was a Friday afternoon when I broke my nose, and I was at the hospital all day Saturday, but there was still no money. The doctors informed my parents that if they did not get the fifteen hundred dollars within the next three to four days that I would never be able to breathe through my nose again.

When Sunday morning came around, my parents decided we were still going to go to church. After the message, everyone was asking me what I had done to my nose, and I told them.

It was very customary for Irma to ask the kids if they wanted her to pray for them. That morning I asked her to pray to heal my nose, I never told her what I had done to it, but she agreed that it would be healed and I would not have to go back to the doctors for surgery. We left church that day, and I could hear my parents arguing in the front of the car about coming up with the fifteen hundred dollars. I told them that they did not need to worry about the money because I am healed. They said, "Okay, baby" in a slightly patronizing tone to try and not discourage me, but it was clear they did not believe I was healed.

By this time, my face was almost completely black and blue around both eyes. I could hardly see out of either eye. I could not breathe through my nose. There was not one person that my parents had spoken to that could help them with the fifteen hundred dollars. It had been four days by then, and they were still trying to come up with the money. I told them that there was no need to worry because God has healed me. They asked me if I was in pain, and I told them I was sore but I was doing much better than the day before. By day five, there was still no money. The swelling had reduced from seventy-five to fifty percent and I was in much less pain. My nose was beginning to take some form and shape back.

By day six, which was a Wednesday, they still had no money. They were beginning to wonder if maybe this "God thing" was true, that healing might be taking place. My nose was starting to drastically reduce in swelling, now the yellow, green, purple, and other colors were all starting to show around the edges of my face. I was able to clear my nose for the first time and have some air circulation through my nose. By day seven, my parents were not as concerned about the money that the doctors had insisted they must have. They were beginning to have some internal confidence, even though they were still trying to figure out how to get some money for the surgery. However, they were starting to consider whether or not they should even consider the surgery. So a few more days went by and the swelling and discoloration in my face had almost completely gone away. I was able to breathe through my nose, not well, but I was able to breathe. That continued so that within two weeks, there was no evidence that I had ever broken my nose. My nose was straight, all swelling was gone, and I was able to breathe fine.

A Lesson Learned

I remember that pain being horrible! But to this day, I can't really recall the pain! However, I can remember how it looked vividly. Sometimes, because we have to look at our situations directly in the face, the impression of the pain is bigger than the pain itself! But if you can get past how it looks, it can change.

Prayer

I am not moved by what I see, I am only moved by what I believe and I chose to believe the word of God. I believe that God's word is true, living and powerful! God, I ask you to come and do the impossible with child-like faith! I will you give you all the glory forever and ever, Amen!

CHAPTER 18

Slippery Slope

UP UNTIL THE AGE of around eight, my sins could mostly be classified as mischievous, the antics of a boy, or even the result of ADHD. But then I was introduced to pornography and additional sexual things when I was about eight to ten years old. I remember one of my cousins, who was several years older than me, led me to hang out with people much older than I was. I think the first time that I was introduced to hard porn was when I was about eight years old. I have a partial photographic memory; therefore, I still remember much of the videos that I saw then to this day. I began to masturbate even before the age of seven years old. This had an impact on me over the course of the next twenty plus years.

I began to have sex as early as eight years old, and this is when the major experimentation began. By the time I was ten, I would have had sex with about four girls. I realized at an early age that the curiosity about sex for people is extreme. To many, it is only physical, and it is not about an emotional response. Treating sex this way can cause extreme damage to the emotions without a proper relationship.

This lifestyle continued until I was about thirteen years old, and by then there had been another four or so different girls which had been added to this list. I started to wonder what was wrong with me. I thought I must have had something wrong with me to have that much of a sexual desire. It started to become increasingly more twisted.

When I was almost sixteen, I remember walking to the store and seeing a transvestite there by the side of the road. I remember him freaking me out. He showed me all of his private parts by flashing me. The part that really bothered me is that I remember not being able to get that image out of my head. This made me think I must like that because I could not stop thinking about it. This perversion of my thoughts continued over the next year to such a point that I began to push a young boy that lived just down the road to experiment with me, even though he was about four years younger than me. This was the beginning of a time where I believed that I must have been gay, that I was a pervert and that I had some real issues. I remember being somewhat pushy with this kid to try more stuff, to go further, to push it just a little more. The effects that this had on me would be absolutely devastating over the next several years.

The shame and accusations from the few that I would tell about myself would be absolutely overwhelming to me. I remember how even though nothing was forced and we did not actually do anything, I still could not forgive myself for the next fifteen years. Over the next several years, I would think things like, "just kill yourself, you would be doing everyone a favor", and "no one needs someone like you in this world." In the next years I wondered how perverted I must be to push myself on someone younger than me.

A Lesson Learned

One of the things I have learned about sexual perversion is that it is very subtle because it is a twisting of the truth. One of the things that the devil has learned to do is convince you of things that are not actually factual. I remember some of the phrases that convinced me I was gay. I was very vocal when speaking with my hands; I would tilt them just a little too much when I would rest them or when I would talk. I was a little too much like a girl apparently... so I must be gay, or that is what many other people would chime in and tell me. My voice began to crack very bad when I was about seventeen, and I had a very high-pitched voice. Though I would eventually get a much deeper voice, at the time it made me feel girly. I also liked playing with dolls, and many other feminine things, so that made me feel girly too. My dad was the type that liked to pick on you, and he would sometimes pick on the thing that bothered you the most – so he had nicknamed me Shawnaria. I hated this for about ten years, but it did teach me to not get mad at people who were just picking on you or trying to get you fired up. I also liked pink and bright colors at the time – I thought that meant I must be gay. People will attempt to tell you that something is wrong with you or that you are supposed to be a certain way. Liking bright colors or thinking a guy or girl is handsome, pretty, or attractive, does not define who you are. This does not determine your sexual preference. Just because you have bad thoughts does not make you a bad person. It is a thought, a perversion or twisting of the truth that the devil is trying to get you to believe. You affect everything in your body by how you think. You can change your taste, emotions, and preferences all by your thoughts. The bible simply says: As a man thinks so is he! This is very evident in the Bible, but it has also been proven in the secular community.

Prayer

God, I repent of things I have done. I ask for your forgiveness, and I receive it by faith. According to your word, if we confess our sins, mistakes, misjudgments, you are faithful to forgive us and cleanse us of all unrighteousness. I thank you for your forgiveness. I pray that I will meditate on the things that are good, pure, kind, and gentle. These are the things that you say that I am. I am hand crafted by your love and grace towards me; you love me, not all of my goofiness, but me! I pray that you would help me change and see me the way that you see me! I know the plans you have for me, plans of success, joy, and peace in Jesus' Name!

Car Accidents

I HAD MY FIRST car accident when I was sixteen years old. My parents had sold me their 1984 Toyota Celica GT Viper for about four hundred dollars. It was white with a cobra on the front right side. That thing might as well have been a Ferrari to me. It was a very sporty looking car. My cousin Sunny and I were driving, and she was not familiar with driving a stick shift. She was the same age as me, so I thought I would be the good cousin and let her drive the car. This was with no license, insurance, or permission, of course.

So she was driving down the road and was doing pretty well overall. We lived in a pretty rural area so it was always a twenty mile drive to get anywhere. Now one thing that is pretty typical in Eden, Georgia is that it rains, a lot. So most of the time, the shoulder is a little soft from all the rain. She swerved just a little off the road, and the car tires caught some of the soft shoulder. It immediately pulled the car to the right, off the road, into a slow sleep bank. We went off the road about four feet, and she over corrected the car to the left. Then we shot across the road while several cars were coming towards us in the opposite lane. We missed oncoming traffic, with what seemed to be only by inches, and then we went off the road on the left side, swerving and stopping sideways. After several minutes of getting our composure back, I got into the driver's seat and we went home. My dad noticed the grass in between the rims and tires and the left two tires going flat. He asked me what had happened, and I informed him that we had slid just a little off the road. He didn't buy the story, but we stuck to our guns; I would not tell him the truth for ten to fifteen years. I only had that car for about six months.

I was working at Ryan's Steakhouse during the summer, which was about forty-five minutes from where we lived. My mom was a waitress for the company at the time, which she did for seventeen years. I was coming home from work and something happened with the water line to the radiator. All the water leaked out in apparently just a few minutes. Then the engine began to overheat and seized up. I pulled over to the side of the road because there was smoke coming from underneath the hood of the car. When I opened the hood, the smoke was immense. This would be the last time that I drove that car.

About one to three months later, my parents helped me get my next car ,which was a 1992 Ford Fiesta. I got it at a used car lot for seventeen hundred dollars. It was basically like driving a roller-skate on wheels. Georgia is a pretty flat country, but you would have to hit the gas as much as you could. By the time you got to about eighty miles an hour going down a hill, you would only be doing about fifty by the time you reached the top of the other side. This was not the rolling mountains of Roanoke, Virginia and definitely not like the Rocky Mountains. These were man made sand hills, and this car could barely make it up them. It was a very compact car.

I was working at Hardy's in the evenings after school which was about twenty minutes from where I lived. This was incredibly closer than some of the other jobs that I had already had. But this one particular day, my mom had gotten up before me to do our lunches for school. She told me,

"Shawn, I was praying this morning, and I really want you to be super careful on your way home today. Make sure you wear your seatbelt and be careful when you get off work." Her telling me things like this was not typical, but me being seventeen, I quickly dismissed what she had told me and didn't really think about it the rest of the day. So I finished out my school day, changed my clothes for work, and off I went to work. We had a general rule that she did not want me working past eleven o'clock because I had school the next day. If I was going to be late, I had to give her a call so she would not worry. Well, it was about ten forty-five, and I was still about twenty minutes from home. I knew I was going to be late, or later than my mom would have been happy with. So doing what almost all seventeen year olds think to do, instead of just calling my mom and telling her I am running late before I left, I punched the gas. I was driving home about eighty miles an hour, in the dark.

Many times the store manager would let me bring food home. I would take the food to my cousins because they did not have much of a budget for food at that time. So on this particular night, I also remember that I had some chicken, mashed potatoes, and some peach cobbler in the car. That peach cobbler was like super glue. It was about impossible to get off things when that syrupy sugar would attach itself to counters or anything else. The peach cobbler turned over in my car, probably because I was doing eighty miles per hour whipping around all those roads. So I reached down to the floor to pick the cobbler up, while I was driving.

That is when I drove off to the right side, hitting the shoulder of the road. I hit that soft shoulder just like my cousin had, causing my car to be pulled off the road to the right side. I then corrected my steering and got back on the road just barely. About three to five seconds later, my left front tire blew out, sending my car back to the right into the ditch. This started my car into uncontrollable flipping. I remember in the midst of one of the flips saying, "Jesus, help me." I also recall that because I did not have my seatbelt on, it was as if I was floating in the center of the car as it was rotating. So I stood up in the seat, pushed my back against the ceiling, and grabbed the steering wheel with both hands, pinning myself to stop myself from flipping so uncontrollably around in the car as well. I estimate by the rotation and the damage, it flipped about ten times. The car finally stopped flipping. The Fiesta was very much the shape of a boxy Toyota Scion you would see today in two-thousand eighteen, before I wrecked.

The front of the car appeared to be pushed under, with the front being shaped like a triangle instead of a square. The right door was pushed in about one to two feet. The right roof was touching the bottom of the door window. The interior mirror was missing. The back of the car roof was touching the bottom of the window in the rear, which had also been totally crushed. Both front tires were pushed underneath the car. I was still conscience, and all I remember thinking is, my mom is going to be so mad at me for being late.

Figure 1: Image by Edmunds.com – This was a similar car to what I wrecked.

I couldn't get out of the car door on the left side, so I used the handle on the door on the right side and was able to kick it open and get through it. I started running home. I was only about one mile from the house. I knew that I could make it in just a few minutes. I had so much adrenaline in my body, it was almost overwhelming. I was about half way to my house when I saw someone in a truck with his lights on yelling. Moving and turning his truck to get the lights to point into different directions. I realized that he was looking for any survivors, so I ran back to him. I told him the phone number to my house and asked him if he could get my mom. I said to tell her that I was having some car trouble. I told him not to say that I had been in an accident, just that I had car trouble, that way she would not wake my dad. He agreed and called my mom. About five minutes later, my mom arrived. She was asking me what was going on, and I informed her that I had gotten in a car accident. She asked me where my car was, and I pointed to it. About that time the police, fire trucks, and ambulance all showed up.

They left the car there until the next morning. The tow trucks came and brought it to the house while my dad was at work and I at school. I tried to act like everything was normal because I already had a reputation of messing everything up and I didn't want to get picked on more by the kids. I remember making it through about the first three periods before the pain started to kick in. I had six abrasions on my back and a one-inch circle cut on my left knee, which I suspect was from the crank used to role the window up and down. I had not told anyone about the wreck. About noon that day, I was hurting so bad that I had put my head on the desk. Sleeping was not allowed at school at all, ever.

So, my teacher was very mad at me and told me to wake up. I essentially told her no, I was not feeling well. She insisted that I get up right then. So I packed my stuff up and walked out of her class without telling her a word. She was yelling at me to get back in her class, and I just looked at her and told her that I was going home. I walked down to the principal's office and told him I was going home for the day. He looked at me and asked me, "Are you now?" I told him yes and to call my mom and tell her I said to come get me. He asked for an explanation, and I just simply repeated: "Call my mom, I am leaving". So he called my mom, and she told me to wait in the car. She apparently explained to the principal what had happened, and I was immediately released from school and did not come back for the next several days. This exposed my secret to much of the school because of my absences. I would spend the next several years having cold sweats and nightmares when I went to sleep. I would relive the accident over and over, sometimes waking up in pure terror. This would continue until I was almost twenty years old, but the worst of it had quit by the time I was eighteen, which was about a year and a half after the accident.

A Lesson Learned

I am fully convinced, based on the condition of the car, that an angel or something came and covered me. The only part of the car that was not bent up was basically right where I was sitting and where I had my back on the ceiling of the car. The left door was pushed in, but the glass was not broken, the front windshield just in front of me was not broken, but almost everything else around me was shattered and crushed! Through prayer, my mom was prompted to give me a warning that I did not heed to. If I had listened that morning, I would not have wrecked at all, however, the power and prayer of my mom protected me from what should have been a fatal crash.

Prayer

Let me know when you are talking to me through other people. Let me hear your advice; bring people into my life that I will listen to, that I trust, and that I know hear your voice. Let me have a deeper relationship with you. I pray that you would help prevent me from being in places that I don't need to be. Let me be the parent, friend, and spouse that hears your voice so that I can lead and guide those around me that you have placed in my care. I thank you for your wisdom and revelation in all situations, in Jesus' Name.

CHAPTER 20

Almost Impossible

MY DAD WAS ALWAYS pretty rough on us, especially to all the people I knew. I have even had several of the relatives tell me,

"I don't know why he wanted to be like that on you guys, after all that he had to go through when he was a kid with his dad". I however, never helped the situation. I had a very smart mouth and an even harder head at this point in my life. I was extremely defiant and refused to do anything that I was told to do. I was sixteen, and it was about two weeks before Christmas. My mom and I tended to get into pretty bad fights. She would get mad at me then for something I had usually done, I would be in trouble, and she would follow me around the house yelling at me. This would sometimes go on for hours. But this day was the wrong day.

She was yelling at me and getting in my face, and I was just trying to stay away from her at this point. I don't remember why we were fighting; I just knew what happened next.

She followed me into the room, and I walked over to the window. Looking out had a kind of calming effect on me. Not allowing me to look outside, she walked up behind me, grabbed me by the shoulder, spun me around, and got in my face to start yelling again. I once again tried to walk away, but she grabbed me again. I turned around and punched the window out, about six inches to the right of her head. Dad came home, and I thought that I was going to be in a bunch of trouble, maybe get another spanking. But this time, he told my mom, you can't be following and grabbing him. He is a grown man; you are going to get yourself hurt. He then came in later and told me,

"Boy you should not have lost your temper that way, regardless if she was yelling and following you. You are gonna fix the window." So we got some new glass over the next few days, and I fixed my bedroom window. This was a mild reaction to the usual ones that I got.

About two weeks later, it was the Christmas of 1997. All should have been well, but my mom and I were at each other's throats first thing that morning. I remember it being really cold out that day, but I don't know what happened to get her upset. I just remember my dad telling me,

"Boy, I know you are mad. You got a right to be; but it is Christmas and you need to put a good face on for the family". So I went outside to an old trailer that we had that we were going to renovate, and I started punching everything there was that I was pretty sure we were going to tear out. I was going to tear it all out with just my fists! This went on for about ten minutes. I came back inside, washed the blood off my hands, and put the Christmas face on. I remember it was an okay

Christmas, but I don't remember most that year, only what would happen over the next few months.

The stress around the house started to get worse and worse. I was getting more defiant by the day and my dad was realizing that a statement I had made several years earlier was accurate.

My dad and I had gotten into it and he had tried to make me afraid in order to control me out of fear, maybe by pain, restriction, consequences, etc. But when this happened as much as it did when I was growing up, I just stopped being afraid of the pain or punishment. I remember looking at him when I was fifteen and telling him,

"You do realize that you can't make me do anything right?" He looked at me and told me he could. I told him he couldn't and that the best he could do was make me regret it. This should let you know why at the age of seventeen I wasn't able to be controlled anymore. But about six months after the Christmas event, the pivotal moment happened. I would make the comment, under my breath,

"You know I could just kill you in your sleep." This was a thought I had many of nights when I had been in trouble, but that day I said it, just loud enough! He heard me say it, and asked me what I said. Knowing that if I lied I would get in more trouble, I repeated it, even louder! He said okay, do it then. He went to the back, got his shotgun, opened it, gave me two shells, and told me to do it!

This was the moment I had been waiting for, for years. To finally be out from under him! He handed it to me, and I knew it was a trap. If I tried to put the shells in the gun, he was going to start hitting me, and if I don't, I am going to get the worst whooping of my life. The only way this actually stops is if I kill him! The problem at this moment was that I realized I could kill him and get away with it by claiming that it was self defense. I would probably spend some time in jail, but many people would rally to my defense. In that thirty seconds to a minute that seemed like an eternity, I realized how easy it would be for me just to kill him. To show him one time he wasn't nearly as big and bad as he thought he was.

I took the gun, turned it upside down, and threw it on his feet. I knew it hurt because he had sandals on. Then he slapped me in the face, and when he did, he fell. I remember laughing, and he got up and slapped me and gave me a spanking, but I don't remember any of it. I just remember laughing! He worked me in the yard for punishment; this lasted for about the next two weeks. It was his custom at the time to make you do hard labor, or some kind of work that would usually last until your hands bled. He would constantly check to see if I slowed down, and if you did, he would have a belt or switch for me and I knew it!

I had met another guy by the name of Shaun when I was about sixteen to seventeen directly before this fight with my Dad, and he eventually came out of the closet to me. He let me know that he was completely gay and that he had a thing for me. Over the next nine to eighteen months, I would begin trying to experiment with him, but this time he was the one that was pushy. This was a point in my life where I thought you were supposed to experiment to find yourself, your sexual preference, and understand why you felt a certain way. We would try some different things over those months, but mostly they just physically and mentally grossed me out. I really believed I was gay and was supposed to be that way even though I just couldn't deal with it.

I no longer had a car because it was wrecked. I had paid off the seventeen hundred dollars that I owed my parents for the second car, and I started making my plans with Shaun to move out. I packed my bags in February, making sure I didn't take anything that could be considered someone else's or belong to the house/family. I waited until Dad went to sleep that night. He usually went to bed early because he got up so early and the pain in his leg would cause him to need the sleep I guess. I never told anyone what I was planning: not my mom, my sister, cousins, just Shaun. I went out the window at about ten thirty at night. I started to hike down the road some and met Shaun at his car. I just walked out, like I never existed. I continued going to school, but I knew nothing else would ever be the same, I could never go back home.

I moved in with Shaun's grandmother and I was not talking to any of my family. It had been two weeks, and my sister lived in Savannah, which was about forty minutes from where we lived. My mom was flipping out because she couldn't find me anywhere. She hadn't spoken to me, and I was nowhere to be found. My sister got involved and had my cousin to watch me at school. My cousin ended up telling her what was going on. My sister told me that she had a room out in Savannah at her apartment that I could stay at if I just kept going to school.

A few years before, my sister had also gotten tired of the crap at the house all the time, so she understood. She had gotten a job when she was about fifteen waiting tables, and she had moved in with my cousins that lived next door to us. They knew how our house was and allowed for this to take place because most everyone thought the crap was messed up and felt sorry for us. But my sister started getting an attitude with my aunt and uncle, so my uncle told her to get out. So she decided to move back into our parent's house. It was never the same for her after she tried to leave, she had to pay rent and was treated like an adult who had to contribute. I remember thinking how she had not left on good terms and I didn't either. So there was no way I was going back to that crap. So I agreed to move in with her. I transferred for the last three months of school. Then it was summer break.

After I moved in with my sister, Shaun spent much of his time over at our apartment. I was still confused about my sexuality but I knew I didn't want anyone saying anything about it. He went to a bunch of friends and told them I was his boyfriend, and that really bothered me. I was not just embarrassed, but I was enraged. We got into it that day; I hit the edge of wall beside the window and broke the bone in my right hand. I told him to get out of the house and I never wanted to see him again. I severed all connections with him forever after that.

I left my house after the big fight, went down to the Piggly Wiggly, bought some Popsicle® sticks and glue, then went to the liqueur store to buy some vodka. The cashiers had seen me in there with my sister multiple times, so they just assumed that I was old enough and allowed me to purchase it. I drank about an eight ounce glass of vodka, and took about six Tylenol. I waited about ten minutes, then set the broken bone in my hand, no doctor, just a dumb, broke seventeen year old. About two hours later, I went to work. To this day, that right finger sticks out just a little unless I pull it in. It's a miracle that I have had no actual issues, or pain out of a break that was set completely wrong.

A Lesson Learned

Sometimes in life you are in toxic situations, toxic relationships, and around controlling people. Sometimes you just have to leave, there really is nothing better you can do! Some people will never change, some will, but it is never your responsibility to stand there and be their punching bag while they figure it out. Those people are never worth what it will cost you in the long run!

Prayer

God, give me the strength to get out of abusive, toxic, controlling, manipulative relationships. Help me to set proper boundaries with people, to know my worth, and to know that I deserve better. Let me discern where you would have me be and when to no longer stay in that situation. I ask for your wisdom and guidance in Jesus' Name!

CHAPTER 21

Not Quite Good Enough

THINGS WERE STARTING TO look up. I was seventeen and living with my sister. I got a job working at Carey Hillards. I would cook and work in the kitchen. There was this girl named Autumn that was a hostess. I had seen her at school some and talked to a guy one of my friends Austin about her. I remember thinking she was so pretty, sweet, nice, and popular. Wow, I thought. So, I would spend time with her while we were at work. We found out that a friend of mine, Shorty, dated her sister. I had met Shorty during the summer. He just seemed to bounce from one house to another like a hobo. He wasn't part of the complex, so he wasn't allowed to swim in the pool because he didn't have a pass.

He was a short guy, about fifteen at the time, and he liked to smoke weed. I had covered for him multiple times that summer, yet I had never actually gotten to know him. I would later find out that his uncle was part of the Mafia, and since he was part of the family, he was to follow suit. He had even been branded as part of the gang with a coat hanger! It was bent into the shape of a dragon and then stuck over a stove until it was red hot. They then held it to his arm until the red had gone out. This was a permanent life brand. He seemed to be the only friend I had since I had moved to Savannah with my sister. We started hanging out often because I finally got Autumn to go out with me.

Life was good. I remember how much I liked her, how I had goose bumps and the butterflies in the stomach, and all those things that go with young love! There was nothing that we would not try to do together. School started back, and she was too busy to keep working at the restaurant. Since she wasn't there, I went and got a job at Tara Cinema. This made me one of the more popular guys in school, because if I liked you, I would sneak you in and get you deals on popcorn. I had also picked a fight with one of the biggest bullies in the school, so I had a reputation. Part of that was hanging out with one of the worst kids in the school.

Autumn's mom was a pretty bad drinker at the time, and there were many nights that she was pretty drunk. So we would sit out on the porch or go to the park that was just down the road and kiss and all that fun young stuff. Everything was good and innocent, but her mom didn't want any part of me. She was a single mom, and because I didn't live with my parents, I was just a bad choice for her daughter! She told her daughter that if she didn't break it off with me, she was not going to pay for her college. Autumn was so torn between the two of us all the time; I remember how much pain and conflict it was causing.

So I made some excuse up and told her we would have

to break it off. She agreed, but we would see each other and couldn't even dare to look at each other because it bothered us so much. I was completely devastated, and my heart was completely shattered. I started drinking almost daily at this point. I would drink every day, and for the next two months of school, I would pretty much give up on life. I had taken some higher English classes in eleventh grade, but they would not transfer over. They told me that I would have to repeat them during the summer of my senior year. When I heard this news, I decided there was no point in staying in school. I spent several days talking to a recruiter for the Navy because my cousin had signed up. I got everything set up; I was just turning eighteen on December 1, 1998, and nine days later, I would ship out to boot camp. I had not told anyone, not my mom, my sister, or my dad. My dad and I had still not talked in almost a year at this point. I had my plane tickets in hand, it was the sixth of December, and I flew out on the ninth. I told my sister and mom that I dropped out and would be leaving in three days. They cried and told me that I shouldn't do it, but I had already made it to where I couldn't have changed it if I wanted to!

A Lesson Learned

There were many of times that I wondered if Autumn was my true love, soul mate, one and only, and all that fun stuff. But what I know is that if I would have stood in that mindset, that many things in the future would have not happened. I am confident that I would have probably not written this book, that I would not have had my current son, and that I would be in a completely different place in my life. I am pretty sure that would not have been a better place than where I am today.

Prayer

Let me forget the things of the past and push towards the mark, the high calling in Christ Jesus! Let me go towards all the things that you have for me, let me trust and believe that you are guiding my steps, just like what David would say in Psalms at the end of his life. Let me believe that, even in the wilderness, you are guiding me to hidden pastures that you have for me!

CHAPTER 22

The New Me

I HAD DECIDED AT this point, everything that I wanted to be, I was going to be! I had been a pathological liar for most of my younger life, usually out of fear of getting in trouble! I was timid, shy, hadn't really done anything, hadn't had any money of my own, and was pretty much terrified of life. I was not ever going to allow anyone to talk down to me, disrespect me, or belittle me ever again! And no matter what, NO GIRL was ever going to break my heart again!

I got shipped off with some other recruits, flew to Atlanta with a four hour layover then flung up to the Great Lakes in Ohio. It was December and we stepped off the plane to about twenty degree weather. I still remember the smell of the street as I went outside to smoke a cigarette after the flight. It was brisk, having a mixture of the clean smell of snow and the smell of exhaust from the cars. About an hour later, a duty truck came from the base and picked some of us recruits up.

Then we were in holding. It was about eight o'clock that

night. We were tired, hungry, and none of us had a clue what we had gotten ourselves into, some less than others. They took us to our barracks and said they would see us in the morning. I remember going to sleep that night hearing several of the guys crying as they went to sleep because they missed home, their mommies, and their family. I laid thinking, why would anyone want to go home?

The next morning began the routines of shaving our heads, getting our clothes, and putting our names on everything we owned. The mornings were supposed to start at six o'clock and go to about ten o'clock at night. It was seven days a week for eight weeks. We would wake up and get ready for muster. I remember how everything was so meticulous, and I remember how easy it came to me. They would make you exercise several times a day, usually about one to two hours at a time. Then usually you would have two to three different types of classes: fire safety, boat safety, swimming, and obstacles courses. The one thing I liked is that it seemed like you never did the same thing two days in a row. Many of the guys would start crying during the exercise, but I would start laughing because the guys would yell. I remember laughing because all those guys were allowed to do was yell. They couldn't hit me or hurt me. That was hysterical to me, so I would start to mess with the trainers we had. We had three different trainers:

Cutter – He was ex-special forces, (Seal) and he had gotten older so he no longer went on missions but decided he would do training. He would come at what seemed to be random times and would work us out. I remember one time he did one armed push-ups while holding a pencil between his pecs! And then did more than most of us could do with regular push-ups! This man was a beast!

Shultz – He was our baby sitter! He came every night and basically watched us while we went to sleep. He would tell us these crazy stories about his time in the military. He had been in about twenty-eight years but had gotten in trouble for hitting his commanding officer that had only been in about two years. So he was finishing his time doing some training on the opposite end of the world.

Reese – I think that was his name, although I don't really remember, but we actually spent most of our time with him. He had gone from a E1 to a E8 in like ten years, which was absolutely exceptional. He was what most would call a lifer, someone that comes to the military, loves the life, and will die in the military! He was a true model of what the military wanted.

So of course Shultz was my favorite because he was a complete smart aleck, and always was making jokes and pushing the rules to the limits. But Reese is who I liked to give the most crap, because he was the easiest to pick on. Cutter told me one time that he was going to break me! I told him,

"You can't break me because you can't bring me any pain that I haven't already gone through". One day, he decided he wanted to cycle me (exercise you until you can't stand up). He said,

"Decker, I'm going to cycle you until I get tired!" So he told me to start doing a combo. These were two jumping jacks, one push up, two mountain climbers, and back up to repeat. So he turned around and headed to the office down the end of the corridor. He got himself a glass of sweet tea and brought his office chair down in front of me and sat down. He called out numbers, up, down, meanwhile giving me a hard time for not doing the exercises right! I felt like I had grown up in this, so this really wasn't that big of a deal to me! It was exhausting but funny to me. This went on for about an hour to hour and a half. He finally stood up and asked me if I was tired yet. I popped to attention and answered, "NO SIR! Would you like me to get you another glass of sweet TEA, SIR?" He laughed out loud and said he was just tired of watching me! I turned around, doing an about-face and passed out! I had learned from being in trouble so much how to push myself past what my body was willing to do, and I had done that. They took me to the emergency room to find out that I had done all that cycling with double pneumonia, and had water in about fifty percent of my lungs. I would fall asleep on watch about three days later, and they would set me back for doing so. I would finish boot camp and move onto graduation, but this was just the beginning of many of my other rebellious acts.

I graduated from boot camp and went to "A" school in Meridian, Mississippi. I would meet several girls while I was there, I would get in trouble multiple times for disrespect and failure to keep a properly ironed uniform. At the time I thought that was completely stupid, so I pretty much refused to do it. I would leave there graduating second in my entire class and with one of the highest grades in that field that had been seen in some time. I was given the opportunity due to graduating at that level to pick my duty station. They had three duty stations available: Alaska, California, and Virginia. So knowing that all my family was in Georgia, I picked California. But I had a buddy that had graduated third, just below me, and he had family in Long Island California and really liked his family. So he conned me into letting him go to California and I went to Virginia. I figured eight hours was far enough from my family that I still didn't have to be a part of anything, or any one of them.

I was done with "A" school and was given two weeks leave. They gave us a free flight to anywhere and then a flight to our final duty station. I decided that I would go home; it had been about six months to a year since I had even talked to my dad for ten seconds. I went home mainly to see my mom.

1999 – The Summer I came back to visit right after "A" School.

I flew in and got there late, about two in the morning. My dad was an early riser and was expecting me. I guess it was about five that morning and I had only been asleep for a few hours. He went into the kitchen to get some ice water to drink. When he turned the water on and shook his glass, I set right up on the futon that was in the living room. I said,

"You better not put no water on me!" It was his custom to do so if we did not get up early enough. He would always shake it to let us know we were about to get the water dumped on us and on the bed! If the little bit of water didn't work, he would get a small bucket and soak me and half my bed! Which by the way, it stayed wet for days. He laughed and said he was not going to do that because he knew I got in late. Well it seemed that everything was going well and looking up. It seemed that we had finally gotten to a point of a mutual understanding. About the fourth day into the trip, Dad told me to get up and go get him a glass of tea. I looked at him and told him, you know you could ask, right? He got mad and repeated himself. I told him I was sorry but that he needed realize that if he didn't learn to talk to me like an adult, he wouldn't see me, my grand-children, wife, or anyone connected to me! That was not the case yet, but I was getting the point across! I told him to get his own tea, left and went and saw my mom at work. I told her I was leaving early and went and stayed with my sister for the last couple of days I had planned on being there.

A Lesson Learned

The only person in this life that can break you is you because the greatest pain you will ever experience will only be in your mind. You will always have to set boundaries with people no matter their relation.

Prayer

No matter what I am going through today, let me see it for what it really is: a thought. Let me deal with this pain, problem or trail by dealing with my thoughts today. Give me wisdom and insight on what to address and when, and give me proper wisdom on how to go about dealing with it.

CHAPTER 23

The Military Life for Me

I GOT TO MY first duty station, AIMD 800. My barracks was about a five minute walk away, so there was no reason for me to ever be late. Petty Officer Farmer was directly over me. You were to be at work at seven in the morning and would get off at four o'clock in the afternoon, every day. Simple, right? Well, not for me. I started to suffer from extreme insomnia. I started going to a bar down the road called The Banque, and I would spend years of my life there. I would basically live in the bars from about eight o'clock to three in the morning every day. I would try to go to sleep, but couldn't. They also had a local rec (recreation) center that we would go to which had movies, pool tables, music rooms, and many other things. I, of course, leaned toward playing pool.

The military life turned into what most say is the life of a typical sailor. To curse, screw, and drink. It started with my obsession with dancing. I had decided, I was no longer going to be that shy, timid, and scared guy. So I would go to this bar called The Banque in Norfolk, Virginia. I would leave there at closing and go to Johnny's Diner. This would become my tradition, every night for the next several years, and I almost never missed a day. I had not yet come out of my cocoon, so at this point, I was still super timid and shy. My cousin said he knew some people and that I should go to that bar. So I did, but all these people he said he knew, I didn't know! And he surely didn't call them and say hey, watch out for him. I would see all the people dancing, but it seemed that I had two left feet and one of them was broken. I had no rhythm, didn't know any of the moves, and seemed that I fit in the typical box of being an uncoordinated, country white guy! So every night, I would go to the bar, get a glass of water, stand in the corner, and watch people on the dance floor. I would occasionally play someone in a game of pool, but other than that, I never would talk to anyone. So there went me coming out of my shell, until one night after about the second week, a girl noticed me.

Nicky. She had blonde hair, blue eyes, and seemed like she didn't have a flaw. She was absolutely gorgeous, and she was walking toward me! I thought, what do I do? I knew she didn't want to talk to me. What would I say?

She looked at me and said, "Hey, you." I was looking around because I knew she must have had the wrong person. But she was pointing at me, and I was very confused by this. She came up to me and asked,

"I see you've been here for the last two weeks and you never talk to anyone, but you always watch everyone dance. Do you want to dance?" I told her I did, but that I didn't know how. She looked at me and remarks,

"I didn't ask you if you knew how, I asked you if you wanted to!" I said sure. She told me to come with her, grabbed my hand, and started to introduce me to every girl in the bar. She told them that if they ever saw me standing by myself, they should go get me and drag me on the dance floor. I was probably every shade of red you could imagine, but I had already decided that I was going to be different. So after that, several of the girls would come up and ask me to dance, and I would attempt to go out on the floor and do anything. This consisted of a lot of slow dances at first. But during the next several weeks, I would notice that all the guys that knew all the girls knew how to dance. So I realized that if I could learn to dance, then it would give me a reason to talk to all the girls. The problem was, I had several girls that were willing to dance with me, but almost none of them could dance either. So I started paying attention to all the girls that could dance. I would go up to them, offer them drinks, and other things, to try to con them into teaching me a dance or some kind of move.

I was learning the country two-step. I don't know how to express how uncoordinated I really was. When it came to bad dancers, I think I was the worst of all time! I got several of the girls to show me how to do the country dance, but one night, Nicky had gotten very drunk and started teaching me the two-step. She was a true wild child. She chewed tobacco, rode bulls, was an erotic dancer, and was in the military. She could out fight and out drink most men I knew but was probably one of the kindest people to me that I knew at the time. She was really plastered and told me she was going to teach me. She came out on the dance floor, with no hands, not even touching, and we went around on the dance floor. I swear, that first six months, I would stay embarrassed, because the only way you got taught was in front of a crowd while you were messing up! But if you wanted to learn, that is when it was going to happen, right then. This became a pattern that would happen most of the time. Someone that was popular would get drunk, and then they would dance with me. Not a real self-esteem builder, but I was still happy that they would show me at least at some point.

I was still working at AIMD 800, and I would go down the hallway, dancing, doing two- step moves, then the waltz, shuffle, the cha-cha, and any other thing that I could practice. It was becoming an absolute obsession. It would consume everything: every thought, every person I would talk to, every place I would go. Well after this all-consuming, seven nights a week, twenty-four hours a day mentality, I was getting good! This then progressed into swing dancing, with extremely complex patterns, throws, and launches. Formal training, of course not! This was just stuff we did on the fly, no instructions, no safety, just pure passion!

A Lesson Learned

Sometimes the only way you will learn something is right then. You are going to look like a fool, a newbie, the one that doesn't know what they are doing. But stick with it, and it will give you a confidence that you can carry into any area of your life.

Prayer

Let me have a passion for things that please you. Teach me how to have fun the right ways, with the right people. Please give me the confidence I need to tackle life, with the passion and persistence to accomplish anything.

CHAPTER 24

My Reputation Proceeds Me

AFTER ABOUT A year, I had earned quite the reputation. I was not only an exceptional dancer, but someone that really was good with the ladies. I was also known to keep my mouth shut. This was the perfect mixture! I had become popular, knew almost everyone it felt like, and I was in the "in crowd" and it seemed that everyone wanted to be me!

One time there a girl I was dating for a little while, and I told her not to do anything behind my back. I told her that, if she didn't like me, she should just break up with me. Well she did, and later brought in her new boyfriend. He came up to the bar and wanted to run his mouth about how he got my girl. So I told some guys I knew to put him in his truck; this meant to hurt him and leave him in his truck, and they were glad to do so! She was told that if she came around with any of her boyfriends, this would happen and if anyone talked to her, this would happen! This lasted for about six months. I had become someone to be feared, with reputation, power, popularity, and I loved it! The girls would come and offer themselves, and I would begin to go from house, to house, to house! I had achieved what most men spend a lifetime trying to have, but now what?

I was also gaining a reputation at work, but this was not a good one. It was a reputation of being always late, resenting all authority; I was dressed sloppy, which is extremely not acceptable in the military. I didn't really like work, or the military, so why go? I had lots of other friends that had done it these things, though many of them had been discharged from the military dishonorably (BCD). However, it never seemed to matter much, or that is what it seemed like. They were fine; they all worked at minimum wage minuscule jobs, nothing of real importance, but were happy as they could be. I began hanging with all the wrong people; many did drugs or were AWOL (which is military desertion). I had a barracks room I was able to go to, that was my room, but I would never be there. I would spend ninety percent of my time jumping from house to house, girl to girl. I started to get to a point that I was only sleeping about ten hours a week. I would many times go two to three days without any sleep. I would wake up having no idea who I had went home with, where I was, or what city I was in. My life was becoming an out of control, uncontrollable blur, with no purpose!

A Lesson Learned

Some of the things that you will pursue the most will cause you the most pain. Fame, popularity, sex, attention, relationships, and money are all fleeting. This is something many of celebrities and others have learned, many times just before killing themselves. Without people that love you and someone to share your life with, what is the real purpose? Many things that you pursue are the reasons you are causing the trouble in your life.

Prayer

Give me wisdom to see what is really important and what is not, and help me to peruse things that are. Let me see the difference between what is good and what is God, what is fun and what is fake, what is my future and what will be my failure.

CHAPTER 25

Still Not Talking

IT HAD BEEN ALMOST a year and a half, and I had not made one call to my parents. Really, this was because of a glass of tea! I don't think I would have ever called home again, actually. I would be that stubborn, with a temper and attitude to boot. But this day was different. I was at work that morning and in walks the CO (Commanding Officer) of the entire base. I believe he was an Admiral, I just remember being terrified because I was almost always in trouble, and when an Admiral comes to talk to you, you're in trouble! Or at least that was what my expectations were at the time. So he walks into one our little offices, and one of the guys yells, "Attention on Deck", so we all stood.

He asked the Senior Chief that was in the room if there was a Decker in the room? He pointed over in my direction, and the whole time he was doing this, he had a cellphone in his hand. Cellphones were not as normal at the time, so to have one was rare to see. I answered, "Yes, Sir!" He said that he had someone on the phone for me. He handed me the phone, and it was my mom! She had tracked down the number of the CO, got his number, and called him. The CO stayed in the room to make sure that I was speaking with my mother. We spoke for about fifteen minutes, and she told me she loved me. I don't remember any of the other parts of the conversation because everyone was looking at me! I finish the phone call, and the CO said, "Decker, I want to talk to you in private a minute." You don't actually get to say no, so we went outside and he said,

"Boy, you're going to listen to me a minute, and this is what is going to happen. I don't take well to a mother calling me. God knows how she got my number. She asked me if someone could tell her where her son was, if he was alive, or anything else! So this is what is going to happen. You are going to call your mother every two weeks and if you don't, you are gonna find yourself with some EMI (Extra Military Instruction, which usually meant you got to do a bunch of additional work). Or you are gonna be prohibited from leaving the base, confined to your barracks, or whatever else it takes to motivate you to call your mom! You got that boy?" There was only one correct answer, "Yes, Sir!" This would be the beginning of me calling home. Just like clockwork, I would call home. Most of the time I would call only when I knew my mom was home. My dad would answer sometimes, though. He would try to make small talk, but I would usually deflect and just ask to talk to mom.

A Lesson Learned

DON'T MESS WITH A PRAYING MOM! You're asking for trouble, especially as persistent and patient as my mom is. That woman is truly tenacious. I wonder if she would have given up if I would have come back home? I may never know, but I do know, if you have someone that you have a strained or separated relationship with, don't ever, ever give up on them! God can do great things because of your persistence.

Prayer

Lord, I ask you would bring relationships that are strained, torn, forgotten or lost back together. I pray that you would be a repairer of the breech and a restorer of the broken hearted and down cast. I ask you to give peace where there was only contention, strife, and bitterness. I pray that you would warm the coldest of hearts and show them a love that only can be understood in your presence.

CHAPTER 26

Fisher – Car Catching on Fire

I HAD A FRIEND named Fisher that I met while I was in the Navy in 1998. He asked me to come with him up to Pennsylvania. I told him that I did not think we should because I had a bad feeling. He persisted in asking, however, but I did not give in.

He said come on man, come up there with me. I restated, "Man, I'm telling you something is just not right". I told him several times that we should not go, but he kept insisting. It was typical for us to go see some girls and do things that we should probably not have been doing. We had this habit of taking a world map and a yardstick and seeing how far we could drive in a weekend. It was not abnormal for us at the time to drive to Pennsylvania or Georgia to see somebody. He reminded me that he was going to go on Friday, but my answer did not change. It was still, "I'm telling you something is wrong." It was Friday and we had a four-day weekend, but I knew for some reason I was just was not supposed to go. He kept insisting and I kept telling him "no", fifteen or twenty times. Finally, that Friday we went out to the smoke pit to kill the last fifteen to thirty minutes of the day and to have another cigarette. It was about three o'clock and he planned on leaving at three-thirty that day. So we were about to finish our last cigarette for the day, and he comes to me and says, "One last time, if you are coming, I am leaving about three-thirty." I told him, any other weekend just not this weekend, next week is fine. "Well, fine dude, I'm gone right after work." He wrapped his things up at work and headed out the office to leave right at three-thirty.

He was headed across a four-way highway that was right near the barracks when a twelve or fourteen wheeler hit the front of his car. It was carrying a bunch of cylinders of oxygen, nitrogen, and many other flammable chemicals. One of those cylinders fell, broke, and released gas that caused his car to catch on fire. He was stuck in the car with this truck on top of the hood of his car. The whole car was on fire and someone saw it, took a fire extinguisher to it, and helped him out. He received burns on thirty to forty percent of his body. The first responders and the doctor told him that if someone had been in the right side of the car, they would have died. I wasn't there that day! I definitely wasn't following God at that time in my life, didn't know the voice of God like I do today, and I never heard an audible voice. I didn't know anything like that; I just knew that I wasn't supposed to go on that particular trip that particular day.

A Lesson Learned

My friend did recover, but he had suffered extensive burns. It took him almost two years to recover from the smoke inhalation, skin grafts, etc. So many times God's grace, mercy, and gentleness is right there to help us through every situation, but we don't listen. We believe we know the direction we should go, but against every friend, counselor, or recommendation, we choose to go a different way! Who has God put around you today?

Prayer

God, let me see the people in my life that are trying to warn me from horrible situations, even if they seem small, let me hear that warning. Let me be easy to listen to reason and quick to respond. Let me be sensitive to your spirit that you may lead and guide me into all truth.

She's Different, but I'm Not

THERE WAS THIS GIRL working at Johnny's Diner. She mostly waitressed but would do some cooking too. She was kind of shy, but she was working at the wrong kind of place to be a shy girl. Johnny's was where the bar crowd gathered at every night. We were a rowdy crowd, so being shy and a push over just wasn't gonna work! So a buddy of mine, Tex is what we called him, decided he was going to hit on her and see where it went. He went over to her and told her she was "looking good." She instantly looked at him and told him to take his little flirting butt and go sit back down! The first thought I had was, dang! He just got shot down. Now that is the girl for me!

This is where I met *the* girl. The one. She was in great shape, knew how to call me on all my bull, and could see right through the entire pretense that I would put on. She worked at the diner that I would so often go after the evening at the bar. I would spend hours there every night and even some of the morning. I was also relentlessly persistent. So we started talking. After just a couple of days when she was getting off work one morning, I told her I would give her a ride. So I borrowed a buddy's car and gave her a ride home. While we were outside her apartment, I leaned in to give her a kiss and she put her finger on my lips and said, "no you don't." Then she gave me a hug and went inside. I hadn't really had many girls do that to me, so I liked her all the more!

At that time, I was still jumping from house to house, but I was getting to a point where I did not want to mess with other girls. I liked this girl; she was the one! So she and I start dating; I would go over to her house, she would shower, and then we would joke, lay around, kiss, and then I would go to sleep. But I also stopped going to work! I was AWOL; I was turning into the friends that I had. I would spend every waking second with her. But her mom hated me! To her, I was just some little punk kid that was messing with her daughter. So it seemed that history was repeating itself. Her mother told her that if she did not stop seeing me, she would throw us out. But we were in love and would not break up, so she threw us out! It had been about twenty days at this time, and I still hadn't been back to work. Things were getting more serious with me and her. She convinced me that I should go back so I did. And her mom let her come back home.

When I got back, I was sentenced to twenty days in the brig with an additional twenty days of restriction where I could not leave the base. But my girl, Shi, came to see me. I was amazed that she was willing to, so I did my time. Everything seemed like it was looking up. The only problem was, I was still not sleeping that much. However, for the first time in some time, I was beginning to love life again.

Because of my consistent tardiness, I was staying in trouble at work. Shi was still working at the diner and Shelle, who was a friend of hers, worked with her. She had been with us when we got thrown out by her mom. She loved smoking pot. After about thirty days of being out of the brig, I decided that I was going to start doing some of that pot with my new girl. We start smoking pot pretty much every day. But all it seemed to do was keep me from going to sleep. This happened for about two weeks, and I figured I would not go back to work. We had been together at this point for about six months. I was spending all my time over at the house. Her mom still hated me but was now at least tolerating my existence. But I just couldn't sleep.

So once again, I got in trouble for my consistent tardiness and decided I was not going back to work. AWOL once again. This time it lasted about thirty to forty-five days. During this time, things were getting serious between Shi and I. So serious that I was getting nervous about how much I liked her. So, I did the only thing that I knew to do: go to the bar to blow off some steam! I saw a girl I knew, and we talked about all the crazy stuff that was going on in my life. We then took a walk later that night down by the baseball field. We started joking and picking and everything, and way led to way. We ended up having sex in the park.

The guilt was absolutely unbearable, so just after a couple of days, I told Shi what happened. She was infuriated as anyone would expect. She said she did not know if she could ever trust me again. I begged her to give me one more chance, and she did. After about a month, things were much better. She was laying on the blow up mattress that she had as a bed, and I rolled over and told her,

"If things work out or not, I will take care of our kid if you get pregnant. But I want you to marry me!" She looked at me and quickly answered no. I asked her again, and the answer was still no. I asked why, and she wouldn't respond. I asked her to marry me again, and then she said yes! We had been together about nine months, and we were getting married. She didn't like a lot of people, and I had pretty much stopped talking to anyone too. We went down to the local court house and got married. Just me and her! I had gone to Walmart and got her a marquise cut two hundred and twelve dollar wedding ring. I promised her that after I got out of the military I would get a real job and get her a real ring. She didn't want me to get out, but I didn't want to stay in. Just a couple of days after we got married, she informed me she was pregnant. I was so excited, but was scared. I was AWOL; I had no job, no insurance, and no money! What were we to do?

A Lesson Learned

You may be at a time in your life where you feel like nothing is going like you expected, with a person, situation, or place. Maybe you are in something you never wished to be in. But it is here, so what do you do?

Prayer

Give me wisdom, Lord. Let me correct wrong things, give up old things, and give me the strength to address the problems ahead and push past my past so I can change my future.

Going Back

MY MOM AND I had started talking, but I knew I should not tell her what was going on. My mom always had a phrase when I was growing up, "If you do something and go to jail, don't call me, because I am not bailing you out. But if you didn't do it, call me, and I will sell everything I have and do anything to the ends of the earth for you." Well, I knew I was, and I had done it.

I decided to go back to the Navy and face the consequences. So I went down to the diner, where there was almost always some MP (Military Police) in the evening, and I told them that I was AWOL. So I got a ride back to the base and started the process of getting in trouble, going to the brig, and getting kicked out! That is what I had wanted, but the MP's wouldn't take me in; I had a reputation and this time, they were not going to be a part of it. They told me to find my own way back onto base. So I did the only thing that I knew to do; I went back to my AIMD 800 office and talked to Master Chief Montgomery. He was an old African American guy that had been in the military for about thirty years at the time and had been through the prejudice of the military and had made it all the way to the top of the enlisted. I sat down in his office, and he asked me why I came back.

There were a couple of answers to this question. One of them was that the JAG officers had called my mom about three days prior and my mom had called me. They told her that if I didn't turn myself in, they were looking at charges that would put me in Leavenworth. The United States Penitentiary, Leavenworth (USP Leavenworth) is a medium-security United States federal prison for male inmates in Northeast Kansas. The charges were real; they said that I had fraudulently enlisted. This could land me there for ten to twenty years, especially with being AWOL for the second time on top of it. This was a very serious issue, so my mom called me frantically, telling me to turn myself in because they were asking if she knew where I was. I had not told her where I was because I knew she would not lie for me. The reasons for the court-martial and fraudulent enlistment charges were because I had dropped out of high school and had not received my GED. The other reason for returning was that my brand new wife was pregnant! This was the first reason I had in a long time to even wake up in the morning. One of the other reasons was that I had promised her that I would take care of my son. I had wanted a son since I was fifteen. To make things right, to do it different, the way I thought it should be done.

Master Chief Montgomery looked across the table and said,

"Decker, this is really simple for me. I can transfer you to a different squadron, or I can recommend you to be kicked out of the military. It is really that simple. What do you want me to do?"

I think this was the first time someone had asked me what I wanted in a pivotal moment of my life! I looked at him with the most sincerity I probably had in some time and told him,

"I just want to take care of my son." My wife had wanted me to stay in, but at this point, I didn't know if that would happen. Everything I had been after was now right in front of me, and I didn't want to make the wrong decision anymore. I had to go in front of the Jag and fight the charges that I fraudulently enlisted.

My mom came to my defense to state that they did not tell me I had to have a GED to enter. This removed the ten to twenty year sentence from the table, but they still had to deal with the last AWOL event that had taken place. They said the only way they would allow me to stay in is if I saw a Doctor/Psychologist and took some drugs to allow me to sleep. He also prescribed that I was not allowed to switch between watches all the time, as it was screwing up my sleep patterns. They would have to put me on three different drugs before I would get to the point where I could sleep through the whole night. But for the first time in years, I was getting sound sleep. I was released from the Brig again after forty-five days and transferred to cleaning duty away from everyone. There was no authority to check in with other than Master Chief Montgomery. There was no boss, no clock in clock out, no uniform. I just needed to get my work done and stay out of trouble. This was to finish the last several months of my duty station, then I would be transferred to my new squadron for a fresh start.

A Lesson Learned

You will always be faced with a pivotal moment in your life, one that can change the outcome forever. Seize it, at all costs.

Prayer

Let me see to seize the correct path so I can have a new and godly life.

CHAPTER 29

New Life, New Wife, New Child

IT WAS JUNE 19TH, 2000, and my wife was very pregnant! She was due on June twenty-third , but we were scheduled to ship out on a six-month deployment on the twenty-second. So the clock was ticking.

Much of the family had come to see me off and give her baby shower items since she was due in a few days. She had given me a box to open with a gift in it, but it would not open. She had bought me a cheap Swiss Army knife a few days before, so I tried to use it to open the present. It was so dull that I was holding the back of the box and pushing toward my hand. It should have been safe, but because the knife was so dull and I was pushing so hard, the box turned. I cut my finger to the bone. It was the pointer finger on my left hand, and I was cut between the first and second knuckle. My mother-in-law was a MA (Medical Assistant) and had been in the medical field for twenty plus years. She got me over to the sink so she could see what was going on. She grabbed some of the paper towels that were there and started to squeeze it to see how bad it was. After a while of trying, she realized the bleeding was not going to stop. She told me that I needed to get stitches. Well, us country boys don't get stitches, unless you are newly married to an Italian wife, then you do what she says!

So we head down to Five Points where the local Norfolk base hospital was. I told the girl behind the desk, what happened, and she told me that she had to check vitals before she could look at it. I guess because I was not overly excited, she didn't believe I had really cut it that deep. She grabbed my finger and was going to cut all the paper towels loose. I realized at this point, she didn't have anything to cover it, and I knew it was going to start bleeding again. I told her she needed to get supplies, and after first declining, she decided to get up and get some. She took the scissors and started to cut on the paper towels, but she never bothered to even ask what side the cut was on. I told her to give me the scissors and get some gauze pads out and be ready for when I got it cut off. She did what I asked but didn't believe that it would be bad.

A few seconds after she got it off, blood started squirting in her face and everywhere else. She started to flip out because that is a medical personnel's worst nightmare. It goes in her eyes, mouth, all over her uniform, and she was hysterical. I reached down, got some gauze, and start wrapping my finger back up. When she was done, she told me that she was going to have to send me to Portsmouth Medical, which was the main military hospital near my location at that time. I was going to need stitches. This was comical in a sense, but now we have to drive thirty minutes at 12 o'clock at night to get to this other hospital and wait.

We go there, and they send me to one of the triage check-in personnel. He asked me what was going on, I told him, and he came back with what it seemed like the entire medical closet. They got the supplies all ready, set it out on the counter, asked me what side it was on, and cut about half way into the gauze before they realized they would just leave it on. It had already soaked through half an inch of gauze in thirty minutes. He told me I needed stitches, but I had to wait for them to begin.

At that point, I was getting very sick to my stomach because of not eating, the pain, and the blood loss. They finally got me into the back. They did a water cleanse on my hand, which was indescribably painful. They open up the wound as far as they can, then shoot water into the cut as fast as they can to wash out any trash, bacteria or loose flesh. Then they take a tissue and shove it down into the wound so they can see the damage and depth of the wound. They realized I had cut it to the bone but did not damage any of the nerves or tendons, which by itself was a miracle. It all hurt so bad that I had taken the aluminum bed frame and bent it with my bare hand, actually twisting the metal. Then I passed out, falling forward onto my face either because of the loss of blood or pain, which one I don't know. They come get me and now on top of all this, I now have a sore face and a split lip.

My face hurt, but they got me back on the bed. I was lying down, and they get the guy with the needles to come. He numbed my hand up so they could give me stitches. He used one of the smaller needles to put an injection in, but about a third of the way through, it broke. So then they had to get a guy to get a pair of pliers to come and pull the needle out of my hand. The problem was, none of the medication had kicked in yet. I pretty much felt everything. After that, they got the needle removed, finished numbing me, gave me some stitches, and told me that I could go home.

That same day, I had to check in for duty at my new squadron. It was about five in the morning, and I was to be there at six thirty. So I drove to my new squadron, no sleep, brand new stitches, no food, in pain, with some kind of splint on my left finger to protect my hand until the stitches heal, and off to work I went.

I checked into my new squadron and tried to tell them what had happened, but no one seemed to care. They told me that maybe they would let me go home early, but we had a lot of packing to do to get ready for the six-month deployment. I was very whiney that day, but at about three that afternoon, they let me go home. I went home, slept for about four hours, and Shi woke me up so that I could go back to sleep in a few hours during normal times. I spent some time with her and went back to bed about eleven o'clock that night.

The next day was the twenty first. I spent the next sixteen hours working, getting everything ready to be put on the ship for the six-month deployment. I had never been on a six-month deployment, nor had I been away from someone I wanted to be with. It was a long day that day and the CO, Captain Richardo, said that if we got everything taken care of, we could spend the twenty second at home all day with our family. So we got done late that night, and I remember being so nervous that my wife had not had our baby yet. It was the twenty second, and the baby was expected to be born today. We knew that this was just a projection by the doctors, but we were hoping that it would be that day. I had gone to the

CO and asked to be allowed "Baby Leave," but I was not senior enough in the command and was not allowed permission to stay. Baby leave could last up to two weeks, or at least until the baby was born. He let me know that as long as everything went well, he would make sure that I would be the first one to come home so that I could see my son.

On the morning of the twenty third, it was six o'clock in the morning and we had to be ready to go by seven o'clock in the morning. I got a cab, went to the base, and then headed to our ship. I had been on a friend's ship where they led me around, but I had never been on one I would spend six months on. It was CVN 73 an aircraft carrier. This thing was massive, having a capacity of fifty-five hundred people, ninety-five feet from the flight deck to the water line. The carrier held about one hundred aircraft in total. This thing was a moving city! I was a little nervous about my new command, but I was mostly just nervous about leaving my new wife with our unborn son. We left at about noon. We were still close enough to shore that we could call all day, so I spent much of my time talking to my wife and seeing how she was doing. Everything was going good today. She was nesting and changing everything around in the house, which seemed to be a weekly habit, even at nine months pregnant.

It was now the twenty fifth, and I was working in the ready room. Petty Officer Farmer has just been transferred to this command as well. I had been told to move a bunch of boxes from the hanger bay to the ready room, so he walked with me down to the hanger bay and said he had some news. I asked him what was going on, and he said I needed to call my wife. The Red Cross called and said they were experiencing some complications. My son had an innocent Patent Ductus Arteriosus (PDA), and my wife had some internal bleeding that they have not been able to get stopped. I told him I wanted to go call my wife. He looked at me and said, we are in flight operations right now, and you are not allowed. I asked him if the phones still work during flight operations, and he told me they did. I turned around and started walking off. He asked what I was doing and I told him I was going to call my wife! He said I could not do that, but I said that he could not stop me. I went upstairs to the ready room to call her, and another lieutenant tried to stop me. I then took a tail hook bar (which typically weights about one hundred and fifty pounds) and looked back at him and said, I'm calling my wife!

The Commanding Officer walked into the ready room right as I had said that and asked what was going on. The LT told the CO what I had said, and the CO looked back at the LT and said "I recommend you let the boy call his wife".

I finally got to speak with her and found out they had gotten the bleeding to stop. I also got to hear my son make a few noises and found out he was fine as well. The CO waited till I was done, then asked me to come in his office. I knew I was in trouble! I saw my file on his desk; it was about an inch thick from most of the things I had gotten in trouble for, and it looked like he had been reading it. He talked to me a minute and then threw the folder in the trash can. Then he asked if we could make a deal. I turned my head and looked at him; he said if I had any problems to come to him and talk about them, and I agreed. He knew that my wife meant so much to me and gave me permission to call my wife every week, no matter what. Also, if there were any problems, I could talk to her. This made this man a hero to me! I became an almost model sailor, everything except making sure that my clothes were perfect. I would have five point zero on all my evaluations, but when it came to personal appearance, I was lucky to have a three point zero. This was an improvement for me. I started gaining rank for the first time, got put in charge at some of the night shifts, and during this six-month deployment, I received several awards and accommodations for excellent behavior, workmanship as well as other things.

A Lesson Learned

That CO was a lot like Christ that day. He took all of my failings, all of my mistakes, my entire past, and just discarded it. I had been around many church circles my entire life and seen very few people ever do something like that. God's grace and his favor gave me mercy. I knew I didn't deserve it, yet I still received it anyway. Not everything worked out the way I wanted them to, but they did all work out. Because of one man's compassion for a boy that was in love with his wife and missing his kid, my remaining time there was changed!

Prayer

What random act of kindness do you have the power to give? What forgiveness can you give to someone undeserving? Lord, show me how I can make a difference, how I can sow mercy, how I can sow grace. I ask you to give me a new start, a newness in life, a new fervor to start the day. I thank you for your grace and mercy, Amen.

CHAPTER 30

Traveling the World

I WAS DOING REALLY well, starting to make friends, and having several guys take me under their wing. I worked with the guys pretty much all day. I was probably ten to twenty years younger than all of them, but they treated me just like I was family. We would go to ports, and they would show me what to do, how to stay out of trouble, where to go to have the most fun, how to make the best trade deals while I was overseas, and things I could do on the ship to make a little money that wouldn't get me thrown in jail. We would go to thirteen different ports and twenty-seven different countries. Countries included Turkey, Iran, Iraq, Egypt, Italy, France, Spain, Portugal, etc. Sometimes we would get to a port and just pay a taxi driver to drive us around all day to go to different countries and eat different foods.

About four months into it, it seemed that my wife and I just all of a sudden stopped talking. It went from talking every day, to only hearing from her about every three to six days, to fourteen days. It seemed like I had lost her. She would not return emails, and every time I talked to her, she was just so angry. She started accusing me of screwing everyone on the boat, telling me how I couldn't be faithful, hated me, and how I was a horrible husband for abandoning her and my son by going on deployment! The list of hateful things became more and more. This lasted for the remaining months that I was out to sea.

I ended up getting to go home early; I was so happy to get to see my wife and son and enjoy life again! Since my son was born about three days after I shipped out, they allowed me to go home about two weeks early.

The trip back was so long. We had docked in the lower southern section of Spain. They then put us in a helicopter and flew us about one hour inland with a bunch of our gear we would need to set up when we got back. Then we got on a C130 (Chop Job) and flew to Portugal. We went from one hundred and sixteen degree temperatures on the flight deck to sixty degrees in Aires, Portugal. We stayed the night there and got up the next morning for our flight home, which was fourteen hours, flying from Aires, Portugal to Brunswick, Maine.

I was smoking about two packs a day at the time and hadn't had a cigarette in fourteen hours. This is a problem if you are a smoker! The plane we were riding in was also very uncomfortable. We got to get off for thirty minutes to get fuel, use the restroom, smoke a cigarette or two and maybe get something to drink. I remember smoking a quick cigarette that only took me about five drags to smoke the whole thing. I then went inside to use the restroom, grabbed some scalding hot coffee, and went back outside to smoke another cigarette. I had no gloves, extra hat, or clothes. It was just pure addiction screaming at every part of my body to have one more drag before I got back on.

I called home and asked my wife to come get me from the base so I could come home. She answered and said, no, and that I needed to find a way to get home myself. This just tore me up inside. So, I asked AZ1 Sherrell if he could give me a ride, and he said he would. I remember walking off the ship and seeing everyone with their family, and they were so happy. There were people crying, excited, and enthusiastic about seeing their children, their spouses, and the ones they loved.

When I got home and knocked on the door, my wife came to the door and opened it. She told me, "Do you have to be so loud? The baby is sleeping, I just got him down!" We tried to talk some, but everything was really awkward. I had not been touched in any intimate way for six months. I had slept by myself, and I had no idea how to approach this woman that was my wife but didn't feel like it.

A Lesson Learned

I know there are certain people in your life that you want more from. Those things that happen, they may not be right. But people have free will; they go through things, sometimes horrible things. But no matter what the case is, you have to learn to stay afloat. The boat does not sink because of the water outside the ship, the ship only sinks when the water gets inside.

Prayer

God, you said in your word, above all else, guard your heart. Father, I ask for your help to guard my heart. I ask for your love so I can love like you love, to rely on you. I pray I would cherish the love from others, but not require it, so I can love others like you do! I ask you for your strength today, in Jesus' Name.

CHAPTER 31

Home, but No One is Here

I WAS HOME, AND while there were people there, it did not feel like it. I tried to spend the next several months wooing her and trying to get her to be excited about me again. But everything was different. This went on for the next several months. Because of my past, she didn't want me to even pick up my son. This is because I had told her what I had done when I was younger with the other boy. She was trying to make sure that she protected my son from a pervert like me! There was no affection; it seemed like nonsense at this point to remain in the relationship. She was used to doing everything without me, everything except for paying for the bills. When I would try to mess with her or have sex with her, she would make excuses. She would say she had to take care of the baby, we might wake the baby, I smelled like cigarette smoke, I was disgusting, or she would say she knew I was banging someone on the boat so I didn't need any from her. This persisted for the next several months. It had now been nine months since I had sex with my wife or anyone else.

Later, I had to go out to sea for some blue water quals (qualifications) that they would do every year. So all the squadrons would be on board for about thirty days, and then we come home again. This was kind of a relief due to all the fighting and tension that was beginning to take place. This was not something that seemed to be nearly as a negative as it was a positive, much different than my first deployment.

I had become friends with one of the girls I had known on the boat during the deployment. We talked about everything and had made some jokes about what we would do with each other if we weren't with someone, but this was just joking. There was no belief that any of it would ever happen. We stopped at one of the ports in Puerto Rico, and we got talking, and I told her everything that was going on. I was drinking that night; it was my excuse to help deal with all the stuff I was feeling (not that it helped), but it was the only way I knew to cope at the time. So we drank, talked, and drank some more! She made an open ended comment about how she would be willing to do something, and I quickly agreed. The remaining time we were out, we repeated this process as much as possible.

We returned home, but this time, I was not home. I was mentally with this other girl. It seemed that because I stopped asking for sex or even trying to get it, my wife wanted to have sex with me again. But now I didn't care! I was home, but I was looking for the next deployment, long weekend, or for one of us to be out of town. The fighting started now. I'm not sure who would pick the fight, but usually it would end with her telling me to get out of the house or I would leave. I would leave for the bar and go to the nearest bedroom I could find.

She wasn't the person I left on deployment, and it was the only way I knew how to cope at the time.

From the time my son was one-year-old, I had only been home about half of his life. I would go and be gone for a month in Puerto Rico, then Nevada, back home, then we would seem to get separated. I would get out of the house, and then it would repeat. This would last from the end of 2000 to the middle of 2002 when I got out of the military.

A Lesson Learned

I have learned to cope with a lot of negative things in my life. Things that are not only heart breaking, but paralyzing to many other people I have seen in my life. But there are proper boundaries that have to be set with people, and when you set proper boundaries, you are more likely to pick positive ways to cope with things you are going through. The one I tend to pursue the most is helping others! This keeps your heart right, tender, soft and gentle. Most other measures will only amplify the pain or cause even more trouble in your life.

Prayer

Lord, help me find positive things to do with my life in this negative season that I am in. Let me help others, let me set proper boundaries, and let me be compassionate to never put pressure on other people.

CHAPTER 32

The Time She Met God

AT THIS PARTICULAR point in my life, I really did not want anything to do with God. Despite all the miraculous things that I had seen God do growing up, I hated Him and anyone that said they were a Christian. I did, however, believe that everyone should have the privilege and opportunity to get to know Christ Jesus on a personal level so that they could go to Heaven. Shi had a desire to go to church. I did a little bit of research and decided on a church about twenty minutes from Chesapeake Boulevard in Virginia Beach, Virginia. The name of this church was the Rock Church. She was not so sure about the whole God thing, and I surely was not going to push any of it on anyone. But after going, I believe she received Christ as her personal savior. She cried like a baby. I think this was one of the few times I had ever seen her cry at this point. We went two other times after this within the next few weeks. This would be the last time that I would walk into a church for several more years.

Everything seemed to go pretty well for the next few months, but we eventually went back to the same pattern of fighting. I started attending night school at Tide Water Tech to become a Computer Network Administrator. We were on the outs again, so I moved in with a girl that was about ten years older than me that I had met at school there.

A Lesson Learned

This church would later play several different pivotal points in my life. I would later spend time coming here to pray and attended a conference that allowed for divine contacts. It was a break from the bar scenes that I was trying to avoid because of the addictions to sex, the club, smoking, and drinking. As stated in the last section, this was a good way to replace bad habits.

Prayer

Give me enjoyment for the things you enjoy. Give me your eyes, heart, and let me love the things that you love. I ask you to fill me so that there is nothing left in me that is not you!

Getting Out

BEING SEPARATED FROM MY wife and not in the military, I went back to the bars and seemed to have a different job every two weeks. One day, I was scheduled to have a job interview to be a telemarketer. I was on my way in my little Toyota Celica, 1984; it was small and white, but it ran. It was a little rainy that day, and I wasn't paying attention. I let up off the gas and rear ended a woman, but I didn't hit her going more than a couple of miles an hour. I got out and looked at her car, nothing was broken, dented, or messed up. So I went and checked on the people that were in the car. I asked if everyone is okay, and everyone stated that they were. The woman asked for my insurance and I complied. I didn't feel that there was any issue. Everything was fine.

So I proceeded to my job interview where I ended up getting the job. I was required to wear dress clothes or a suit, so I usually wore the suit. It was the only one I had at the time, and I had gotten it from Goodwill for about ten bucks. It looked pretty good. On my first day, I went through their four-hour training program and then I went to work for the remaining time. I did okay on sales that day and was still enjoying how it worked. By the third day, I was breaking all the rules, wasn't sticking to any of the scripts, but I had some of the highest sales they had ever seen. They offered me a lead position if I would stick to the script, but I knew I wouldn't do that! So I finished my shift, never said a word, and went home for the day without planning on returning.

As I was driving back, I saw some construction guys out working. Because I had grown up around construction, I knew these companies were always a man short. So I walked into the construction office and asked to speak to the foreman or manager for a job. I didn't know it at the time, but I had walked up to the main owner of the entire company. He looked at me and asked if he could help me, and I said that I needed a job. He looked at me in my suit and said I was in the wrong place. I told him I had done construction when I was a kid. He then told me to give him my hand, so I reached my hand out. He flipped it over and said that I did not have any callouses. I told him I would get them. And I have other work clothes at home for doing this kind of work. He asked me if I had tools and I let him know that I would get some out of my first check. "What can you do?", He asked me. "I know just enough to get in trouble, I learn super-fast, I work hard and I'm the best gopher you've ever seen!" He smiled and asked me how much I would like to get paid. I told him that I wouldn't take less than eight dollars, but I was worth ten. He told me to come in tomorrow at eight in the morning. Right at the same time I started school, I then had a job at Gibraltar Construction Company.

On my first day, I worked with a man named Luke. He was tall and slender; it seemed like he had five foot arms. He saw me and introduced himself. He told me what time work started and what time it ended. It was eight to five, every day. I told him I needed to leave at four because I had school and needed to shower. He laughed and asked me why he would care if I had to go to school. I looked at him and told him that I was going to school. But I also said that if he kept me, I would not miss one day of work, I would always be on time, and I would out-work half of his other guys! He answered that if I did not do exactly that, he would fire me on the spot. I agreed.

I was still a gopher, which is really just someone that goes and fetches stuff because he or she does not have enough skills to actually be important. He would send me to make rafters, get wood, and do other things that really didn't require a lot of skill. But if I was to carry wood, I always had to carry more than the other guys to make up for getting off an hour early. If the guys had one sheet of plywood, I was required to carry two, etc. This would become the daily pattern. He would tell me to speed up, I did, and he expected me to keep the pace. And man did he have a pace! He had taken me down to a hardware store and got me some basic tools, belt, hammer, utility blade, and that kind of stuff. I remember he didn't let me get the cheap tool belt either. It was the good one, made out of leather with multiple pockets. I got my check, and they were paying me ten dollars an hour for eight hours a day, even though I wasn't staying that long. He conveniently swung by the store, helped me get my check cashed, then stuck out his hand wanting the one hundred forty dollars back for the tools that I had gotten.

Regardless of what was going on, I went to work and school. I stayed with my roommate for about seven months. I paid my rent, went to bars, clubs, and met girls. This was my everyday life. There was almost no talking to my wife or my son. We were fighting and my patterns were only making things that worse between us. The lady that I had rear ended took me to court, claiming that I had hit her car, caused multiple personal injuries, and even broke one of the girls' wrists. The first trial that I was taken to, they were going to award them over twenty-five thousand dollars in damages. My insurance told me that I would only be covered for about half of it, and I would have to pay the remaining out of my pocket. The first judge was an older African American lady, and she told me that I was taking advantage of the system and that the victims should be awarded for what I did to them. My lawyer appealed the case and a jury was called; it was found out during this one day trial that all the claims had been pre-existing conditions, and that the injuries were fabricated. The second judge was an older African American man, and when the trial was done, he would not allow one dime to be awarded to the group of people. He also made them pay for all court costs, lawyer costs, and inspection costs to the other companies. In this situation, I was being targeted because I was in a suit looking like a business man, but real justice was done at the end of the day.

I finished school at Tidewater Tech, and I was scheduled to graduate with honors. At the time I had a ninety-one point seventy-three average for the year. Because of my GPA, Cisco™, Sony®, and another company had all offered me a job to come work for them. I was very interested in working for either Sony® or Cisco™ at the time. Both had offered me jobs starting at about twenty-five thousand per year, but after about five years, I would be making around forty-five thousand. This looked like one of the most promising moves ever since I had gotten out of the military.

My mom and dad had moved up to Roanoke, Virginia about one year before I had started school. They decided to move to the area so that they could be four to five hours from their grandchild in Virginia Beach instead of eight hours away in Savannah, Georgia. There were multiple lakes that would only be about an hour from the house they were purchasing. It was mountainous with a much cooler climate then the Georgia heat, so it was a much better fit for them as they were getting older. My mom started working for an appraisal company as an office manager. At the time, she was not very computer savvy and most of the work that she was to doing required some type of computer skills.

Danny was the guy that would train her, and he was only about twenty-two at the time. He had grown up around the appraisal industry and only knew one speed! That speed was: as fast as you can. This was the same speed that he would try to explain everything to my mom. The only problem was, she didn't catch onto it that fast. They had moved up to Virginia with no jobs, so my dad came to the office and helped her understand some of the software programs. He was at least twice as computer savvy, even though he had only completed the ninth grade. He came every day to the local office and helped my mom for the next two weeks. The owner was so impressed by his willingness to continue to help that he asked if he had ever done appraisals before. He was interested in offering him a job. My dad informed him that he was not very academic, but Dan said they could still try it out. For the next two weeks, dad came in and watched Dan fill out appraisal reports. Then he started doing some of the forms and, after six months, he progressed to the point he was doing an entire appraisal. A few months later, my sister also began working for Dan.

By this time, I was supposed to graduate. I had two offers that I was very interested in but had not officially taken either one. My mom, dad, and sister were all working for Dan and seemed to be doing quite well. I was telling my dad about the offers I had received, and he asked me if I would even be interested in doing real estate appraisals. I asked him about how much it paid, since I already had two different offers on the table. He informed me that the first six months you can make twice as much at McDonald's© and work half the hours, but after that, you can pretty much make as much as you want to if you hustle. I asked him a little about the job and found out you pretty much work for yourself. I thought that was the job for me.

I told my wife that I was going to Roanoke, Virginia for a job and she told me she would not move there. I was still working in construction at the time and had promised a few more weeks. They were finishing up the job in Portsmouth, Virginia, and I was going to make sure I kept my word to Luke because he had helped me out so much. I informed my wife that I thought it was the right decision and that it would be the best thing for me and the family. If she came, that was great, but if she did not, I understood. She decided not to come with me. I graduated in June from Tide Water Tech and on August eighth, I started my first day doing appraisals.

A Lesson Learned

Not everyone in your life is going to stay with you. This is why Jesus says children, wives, and family will hate you for his name's sake. I knew I needed to go and take the job, but it would be years before I would really learn all the reason why I needed to.

Prayer

God, I ask you to lead and guide me. Let me be led by your spirit and grace. Let me have wisdom to know when I should go and let me keep those that you have given to me!

CHAPTER 34

New Job Doing Appraisals

I HAD NEVER DONE appraisals before. I was twenty-two years old with a baby face and no facial hair. I looked like I was about fifteen years old, and I did not know anything about being self-employed. I was hired on as a 1099 employee making a fifty-percent commission on every appraisal I did. My sister had been working there for about six months, and she was still a newbie to the whole appraisal industry, but she could help me some. My dad was responsible for teaching me and my sister, even though he had only been at it for about a year at the time. My sister made the mistake of saying there was "nothing to it." Because she wasn't good yet, she would never live that comment down. When I started out, I at least knew not to say anything like that, or I would get the same treatment. I thought it, but never made the same mistake. Instead, I made the mistake of thinking I could do it better, faster, and more than anyone else in the office.

I came over to start the new job, and even though my wife

had said she was not coming to Roanoke, she was staying with my mom and dad there. Things had gotten really bad between us, and I was pretty much content with being in any other relationship but my own marriage. But here she was, willing to come and make an uncertain transition for a man that she didn't know if she wanted to be with that was seeing someone else. That night was the first time in almost seven years that I got some clarity about where we went wrong.

If you remember, I said everything seemed different when I had gotten back from the first six-month deployment. It was because everything was different to her. Because, while I had been gone during that six-month deployment; she had some things which I will not explain per her wishes. But to me, they explained the hate towards me for not protecting her, not wanting to have sex, and the bursts of rage. I had not handled most of it properly over the previous seven years, but this at least explained all the massive amounts of things that just seemed out of place. It would explain enough to me that I would give us a fresh perspective. I wanted to give her a new chance: something to work on, some where to start, a new and fresh point for our lives.

A Lesson Learned

I do not know how to express how many horrific things happen to people. People are violated on a daily basis, and this happens in so many ways. I don't know what someone has done to you, but you can't hold it in. It is like a cancer, and it will eat you from the inside out. While it is killing you, it will kill almost every relationship around you. I learned a phrase years ago; it was, "hurt people, hurt people". This becomes even truer the older I become. I have been responsible for hurting so many people in an attempt to avoid how much I was hurt. But like so many, I bottled it inside and let it eat me alive until no life could be seen in me!

Prayer

I ask for you to help me see my hurts, pains, or troubles. Let me see how this might be effecting the people around me. Let me have the courage, faith, and zeal to express the things that I have been through to the ones that I love. Then give me the confidence, faith, and tenacity to outlast the effects of these things that have happened to me or the ones that I love.

CHAPTER 35

A New Start

THINGS WERE SO MUCH different. There was no feeling of separation, thickness in the air, resentment, or hate. Wow, the difference that change in perspective can make! I was kinder and gentler, and she was happier, more passionate, and more open than I had seen in years. This gave us a new hope. Dad had given us about six months from August to stay at their house so that we could save up enough money to get an apartment. Every day for the first six months, I would go to work as an apprentice, and while I didn't make that much money, I did get my training out of the way.

I started to get more money, but I didn't really know how to handle it. I started the first month making about one to two thousand dollars. Then the next month, I made two to three thousand dollars. The following month, I made about three to four thousand dollars. Man, I was becoming obsessed with work at this point, and the money was rolling in. I started covering more and more areas for my job. One of my first areas was southwest Virginia. This included everything from Wytheville, Virginia all the way down to Bristol, Virginia. This was about a two to five hour drive from us. Every bit of it was rural as could be and almost all of it was the worst kind of work. But I was the newbie, the lowest person on the pole, and man did it seem like I was getting the shaft. But I was still making great money. But because I was doing so well and doing so much work, I was given the ability to pick up some additional work in Virginia Beach. So the crazy schedule began.

I would drive down to the southwest Virginia area during the middle of the week, usually on Wednesdays, and then I would wrap up those three to eight reports on Thursday. Then on Friday and Saturday, I would drive over to Virginia Beach, Virginia and do some more work. Most of my Friday's started about four to six o'clock in the morning, and I would do inspections until nine in the evening during the summer months. The inspections would usually start in Richmond, Virginia at about eight to nine in the morning, and by the end of the day, my last inspection would be in Chesapeake or Virginia Beach. I would then go get a hotel/motel for the night and would usually get up about seven to nine o'clock in the morning and proceed to do inspections on the way home. The hours were crazy, but so was the pay. I remember one of the best checks I got; I made eighty-eight hundred dollars for one month. But I would work eighty to one hundred plus hours every week. I was a go getter, doing the only thing I thought I knew how to do.

A Lesson Learned

There is no freedom like the freedom of release. When we release things such as shame, pity, hurt, bitterness, resentment, hatred, contempt, and guilt, it is like a breath of fresh air, as if all the weight is gone.

Prayer

God, I know I have done so many things wrong and that so many wrong things have been done to me. But I thank you that you wash away all my guilt, shame, and bitterness. You make me clean, pure, and perfect in your eyes. I ask that I would focus on what you think of me, and I ask you to put others in my life that show me what you see.

CHAPTER 36

The New Place

MY WIFE AND I did not manage our money well. I was only making about four thousand a month at the time. I was using about one thousand for hotels, food, and gas every month. We spent most of it, not saving, and at the end of the six months dad had given us free at the house, we still had not saved or prepared. So he gave us two additional weeks because he knew I had a better check coming and then we had to be out. So we got a cute little apartment in the central Roanoke area on the lower floor and everything was going great. We started getting things like furniture and all the little things that make a place a home. We had spent most of our marriage living with other people, and it had really taken a toll on our relationship. But everything was going good, and it seemed that I had finally arrived at a place that many people would love to be at.

We had a small Ford Escort and were driving to Valley View Mall. At the time, they did not have a long merging lane to go to the mall, so when you would up the hill and over the bridge, there was not a lot of visibility if traffic had gotten backed up. So, I came over the top of the bridge to see that the traffic right in front of me was at a complete stop, but there were no cars in front of them. I hit the brake as hard as I could and realized I was not going to be able to stop fast enough. So I swerved over to the right shoulder to miss the car that was in front of me. Just as I did that, another guy did the same, pinning my car between the guard rail and his truck. My car turned up on its side, enough that my rear left tire had hit the top of the front of his truck. My wife got out of the car frantic, not only because our only car was totaled, but because her brand new Melissa Etheridge case was broken as well. We turned to my son that was in his car seat in the rear and asked if he was okay. He was said that it was a really crazy ride, and it was kind of fun, but momma just cried and cried and then she cried some more. I don't think momma thought it was all that fun. We exchanged all the insurance information and were able to get the car off Interstate five eighty-one and drove it to the Valley View Theater.

My mom and dad met us there and took us home. They were nice enough at the time to lend us one of their cars while over the next week or so we dealt with the insurance company. The wreck was found to be our fault and the insurance was only going to cover the damages, not any of the replacement cost. So we were out a car after just moving into an apartment. We had been doing well at the apartment and were starting to get ahead. I had about thirteen hundred in the bank. We took every dime we had after we found a little economy car at Enterprise Car Rental. This is when they first got a department to sell them, and we found a cute little Ford Focus. It was not the best situation, but everything worked out, and we went back to our life.

I was doing a southwest Virginia run this particular week, and I never canceled appointments because my schedule was too tight. I would schedule out weeks in advance many times, squeezing every single appraisal I could in so that I could make a few extra hundred dollars every week. But this week it was cold; it was two-thousand three, and I think it was one of the coldest winters that many Virginians had seen. It had been snowing, raining, and sleeting, but I did inspections anyway. We just made due with whatever was going on. But this afternoon, I was headed back from Taze-well, Virginia, and many times, the easiest way to get there was to drive through the West Virginia, Bluefield area. I had made this trip thirty times, so it really didn't mean much. It was mid to late afternoon around two o'clock in the after-noon, and the roads looked dry. You would see the occasion-al dark section on the road where the chemicals they used had melted some of the snow and ice. So I got to the Blue-field, West Virginia to Virginia Bridge, and as I was driving across it at about forty-five miles an hour, my car started to go sideways.

I was about halfway across this quarter mile long bridge, and while my steering wheel was pointed forward, my car was sideways on the road. The wind had hit my car because of the deep ravine I was driving over and sent my car into a spin. I was on black ice, going forty-five miles an hour, and my car was pointing towards the railing to go off the bridge. My car continued to stay sideways while it was sliding and every sec-ond, I was realizing that if my car caught traction, I would go over the side of this railing. It was probably a quarter mile drop to the bottom. There was no way I would survive this if my car went over the edge. As my car was sliding, I was getting closer and closer to where the bridge ended.

I was almost completely sideways on the bridge, and I could tell that the road in front of me was a different color then the bridge, which meant it was dry. This also meant that if I couldn't turn my car into the dry, I was probably going to flip when I hit the road. So I turned my tires towards the road and punched the gas. Just about that time, my tires caught the dry road, and it yanked my car forward. I was driving toward the right side ditch. I was still doing about forty five miles an hour, but now I was headed right toward the ditch. I already knew I was going to wreck my car. I was just trying to ride it out, hoping I did not kill myself or damage my car to such a point that it could not be used anymore. This entire accident probably only took about thirty seconds to happen from beginning to end, but to this day I remember almost every detail as if it was a week-long event.

As I drove off the road, the ditch was about three feet down a relatively sleep bank into a concrete drainage ditch. I was no longer concerned about going over the edge of the cliff, but I was concerned about damaging my car. I went up one side of the bank and down the other. Finally, after what seemed like five minutes, I got the car stopped. The car had a bunch of funny smells, the burnt rubber from the road, the smell of bad or burnt wires, and the smell of radiator fluid. My heart was pounding, not because I wrecked the car, but because it had only been thirty days since I had totaled the other car. The only thing that I kept thinking was there was no way my wife would ever forgive me for this! There was no way she will be able to look at me because of how stupid I was! So I was on the side of the road, and I knew if I called my parents they would come get me. I was about two and half hours from Roanoke, Virginia so I knew I would be there awhile. I was able to get a hold of a tow truck company, and it was going to be about thirty-five minutes before they could even head my way. They already had a lot of service calls because it was so cold. So after about an hour, they were able to come get me and took my car down to a salvage lot in Wytheville. This was only about two hours from Roanoke, and my parents met me there. My mom was gracious enough to call my wife and tell her what was going on. My parents came, got me, and drove me home. When I got home, I never heard one negative word. I remember feeling like the biggest failure that had ever walked the face of the earth.

A Lesson Learned

Sometimes in our lives, we go through a really bad season. Not because it is God's will, but because of our bad habits. Even still, God still provided his protection, grace, and mercy, even though I didn't really see it.

Prayer

Father, I don't know why I am going through this particular season in my life. But I ask you to show me your grace, protection, mercy, and wisdom. Teach me your will through your word. Give me the grace to know the things I can't change, the strength to change the things I can, and the wisdom to know the difference (Serenity Prayer).

CHAPTER 37

Just a Paycheck

AFTER THE CAR ACCIDENTS, everything returned to normal. But I had felt like such a disappointment because of what I had done, I figured I had to make up for it. This is when the hours became really crazy. I was doing several trips a week, driving close to a thousand miles a week for appointments. A typical day was twelve hours a long day would be twenty-two hours. This was becoming my normal. I was never home, but the money was good. We moved to an upper class apartment complex that was really more like a fourteen hundred square foot home with pools, gyms, and free movies. It had three bedrooms and two baths with all the bells and whistles.

We had gotten another car after the Ford Focus, a little used 1984 Toyota Celica. It was a cheap little car, but we paid for it. It seemed like only half the stuff worked, but it was reliable. Everything was starting to look up again. After about six months of this, while on a trip, the car broke down in Richmond, Virginia. My wife was driving me because I had lost my license again for speeding. A really nice older couple helped us get it to a garage, and I got a ride from my dad as we overlapped territories in the same areas. Dad picked us up, and we found out that the car was not salvageable, so we junked the car and went to another car lot. We had been doing much better, so I got a 2003 Ford Taurus with twenty-six thousand miles on it with the low interest rate of sixteen point five percent (little sarcastic). I swore that was the highest interest they could give you on a new/used car, but we didn't have the credit to get anything better. Everything went back to normal, back to work, back to long hours, and back to the bars to give me some kind of entertainment or meaning. The money was great, and we bought everything new, went any place we wanted to eat, and anything the kid wanted, I bought. I was never there, but I bought it all. My wife didn't work and only had a few part-time jobs since we had been married. I was the bread winner, and I was doing a good job at it. We had everything! I had worked my way up the ladder, was covering a lot of area, and was fast at it. This year would be one of the first years I was the highest paid appraiser. I got this title three years in a row. No mistake, I worked for every bit of it!

One morning, I was headed over to Virginia. I had gotten up at about four o'clock in the morning, and was on my way over to the beach. I had a long day planned, and my first appointment was at nine-thirty in Virginia Beach. I needed to get going, but the problem was, Shi and I were fighting again. The night before was a lot more fighting than making up, and we had stayed up until one o'clock in the morning fighting. I remember telling her that we would just have to finish it when I got back. I went to sleep to get up three hours later; this was less sleep than what I typically got, but I still felt like I could handle it. As I was driving over, it was a little cooler so I had my heat on, I had a head ache from the lack of sleep, the caffeine, the bad diet, and the over exerting myself. But this really was my typical day.

I didn't want to have the windows down or the radio on because I just wanted silence. It was just peaceful, no one on the road, the sun was not up yet, and off I went. Everything was good, but I noticed after about thirty minutes, I was already getting sleepy. Most of the time I would just pull over and catch a fifteen minute nap and be a little later, but I couldn't afford to do that today. I had that crazy schedule, so I pushed on. Well, I remember looking down and it was about four fifty something, and I was nearing Lynchburg. I was just getting past the main roads and turn offs, so it was a straight shot of nothing all the way to Petersburg. As I was driving, I remember doing some of the things I would do to wake myself up. But then all of a sudden I heard,

"Shawn, Wake Up! Wake Up, Shawn! Now Shawn, Right Now!" I heard that, and then I looked up and I was driving right towards a guard rail. I drove up on some gravel, slid, hitting some orange caution cones that were there. The cones pushed my bumper in just a little when I hit the gravel and started sliding, missing the guard rail by inches. I got the car stopped and looked around. The sun was rising, and I was almost in Farmville, Virginia. There was no radio on, no cars on the road, and there was nothing around! Who told me to wake up? I heard it like I would if I was in my own bed, but there was no one or anything around. I had driven over an hour and didn't remember any of it. After everything stopped,

I got out of my car, unable to stand because of how much my knees where shaking. Once again, I made it out of something I should have never made it out of. But why?

The importance of this event soon wore off, and I headed back to my typical routines. I was working more than I was home. To treat myself, I would stop at the bar that I used to go to when I was in town. I was always good at doing my work and getting my job done, but my moral compass was completely broken. I would work, go home, play husband and father, and go back on the road. My routine was simple; I did inspections all day Friday, and when I got done, I went to the bar. I would dance, talk some smack, and usually go to the hotel room with someone. I would get up early the next morning, get back on the road, finish my inspections, and go home. The process would then start all over. This was simply my life and would remain that way for the next several years.

A Lesson Learned

Sometimes the worst thing you can do in your own life is just to, simply disengage. You become so tired, that you are not happy or sad, you're home but not present, a parent but not a father/mother. Yet still God was still watching over me.

Prayer

Give me the strength to stay active, and engaged, no matter how hard, not matter the struggle, so it will always give me purpose and principles. Keep me in this time!

CHAPTER 38

Finally Going Back to Church

IT WAS THE FIRST Sunday of 2007, January the seventh. I had not been to church since 2002 when my wife was saved. She had gone several times after that, and she had seemed to be a nicer, kinder, more gentle, and more at peace person than I had ever seen her. I had made a promise to God several years before that; if he would change her, or our marriage, I would do anything He wanted. So as we headed to church that day in the car, I laughed out loud, and my wife asked me why. I told her I would not miss coming to church again. I would have the opportunity over the next three years to really prove this, but these years were some of the hardest years of my life. In the next few chapters, you will see why.

I remember that day going to church because we were greeted by a guy named Joe Mays. He passed away in 2016, not long before I began writing this. I had never been to this church before, but this guy knew my name. I remember him asking how Shi was doing, then turning to me and asking,

"So you must be Shawn then?" I said yes, and I remember being in pure shock that someone knew my name. I would later learn that he had been a mail man for twenty-five plus years and had an excellent memory, and an even more impressive ability to remember names. He had been a green beret in the Army and was one of the kindest, gentlest men I think you could ever know. I began to go to church and listen to the word with more fervor than I had ever had in my life. I felt hungry, like there was a passion that I had never had in my life. For the first time, it felt like there was some real answers.

I remember going to the pastor after just a couple of weeks and setting up an appointment to talk to him. I went into the office to have a conversation with him. I informed him I was there to serve and to be under him. I knew I needed some type of guidance or supervision since I had done a pretty good job at screwing up most of my life at this point. I figured having someone over me couldn't hurt any more than what I had done. So I went into his office and let him know that I wanted to help. He asked me if I liked children. I told him that if he wanted to come in to one of the rooms to find them hanging upside down from the ceiling with a muzzle, then it would be fine if he wanted to put me with the children.

He laughed and said he wouldn't put me with the children. He asked me if I was musically inclined, and I let him know that I was technically tone deaf per what my dad had told me, so that would probably not be a good fit. He asked me if I was any good with computers. I told him I was very good with computers and had actually gone to school to be a computer network administrator. He and I agreed that it would probably be a good fit for me to work doing the slideshow, song presentation, announcements, etc. He asked if there was anything else I wanted to talk about. I told him how I had been called to the ministry when I was fifteen years old, prophetically told by three different people over several months. I had been called from a crowd of people that I had never met. I told him how I had seen God do many things. He smiled and laughed a little, leaned back in his chair and said,

"That is great, but the Bible says to show yourself approved." I remembered that scripture, but I left very aggravated thinking, who does this man think he is? I don't need to prove myself to anyone. I was called when I was fifteen! God had already called me, who did I need to prove myself to? I don't think I have ever actually told him that, but the next year would prove how not ready I was for a lot of things.

I agreed to serve on the Audio Visual (AV) team and started working for a woman by the name of Debbie. Debbie was an absolute firecracker. But within just a few months, she resigned from the position, leaving me in charge of it. This would cause a cascade effect, making me in charge of most of the department for the next several years. You could say from that moment, everything really is history.

During that half a year to a year, we had moved again, but this time to an apartment complex called Heatherwood Apartments in Boones Mill, Virginia. I had quit smoking, drinking, looking at porn, running around, and got really serious about my marriage, God, and being a good father. Much of these things were almost supernatural. The kind where you wake up in the morning and you just don't have the urge anymore. The kind that are just pure miracles and that you couldn't claim you had anything to do with them even if you wanted to.

At the time, I was listening to about eight to fifteen hours of biblical teaching, the word, or other forms of teaching a day. I did this almost every day for the next two years. This was becoming my everyday habit.

I was listening to the Bible one morning, and later that day, my wife stepped off of the front step in front of the apartment. I watched her foot turn completely sideways and around. I was almost positive it had completely broken. She was screaming in pain. I told her, repeat after me, "By His stripes I am healed." She did this for the next few minutes, and her foot began to straighten back out, and she could begin to breathe normal again. There was no longer as much pain. After a few more minutes, she was calm and the pain was only mild; and within about another ten minutes, she was almost completely pain free. I told her to just keep saying that and she would be fine. But after a day of being fine, she started saying; I don't think it was broken, I just think it was a bad sprain. It began to hurt more and more over the next few days, until it ended up giving her a sprain that lasted for the next several months.

A Lesson Learned

When you do radical things, you get radical results. Many times in my life, I have seen a miracle by God, but watch someone's confessions change the outcome to such a point there is no miracle left because of their belief and confessions. I have learned that, at your core, you are full of something! The bible says, "As a man thinks, so is he", so my question is, what are you full of?

Prayer

Lord, show me what I am full of and how I think. Love, Hate, Jealousy, Kindness, Gentleness, Gossip, etc. Let me be full of things that I want to share with others.

CHAPTER 39

Meeting Charles

I REALIZED THERE WERE a lot of things I needed to learn. I was still working like crazy, but whenever I was driving, I would plug in some kind of teaching. I had realized that I needed some help when it came to my finances, and there was this guy at our church that knew a lot of different things about it. I was very interested in that and had seen him do it, so I walked up to him after service asked him if he could help me out. We ended up spending a lot of time together. He was doing several different seminars and other business ventures, and he wasn't that much older than me.

A Lesson Learned

Divine connections and relationships are some of the most precious things that you will have in your life. They will help you, mold you, and change you just because of their presence.

Prayer

Thank you for the people in my life. Let me see them for the impact they will have on me and that I will have on them.

CHAPTER 40

No More Bars

I HAD STOPPED GOING to the bars because I had gotten so much more involved in the church. So to give myself something to do, I would go by the Rock Church to pray. One day while I was there, I saw a poster for the 2007 Consecration (prayer) Conference. I thought this would be unique and cool to go to. I didn't really have the money, but we were not super busy that month doing appraisals. I had gotten an apartment with a friend of mine, which was shared with my dad in Norfolk. This is an article that was pulled recently from the internet to give you an idea about the event:

Consecrations Conference

Virginia Beach, VA, April –Life Coach and best-selling author Pastor Paula White will officially kickoff the Assembly 2007 "Consecration Conference" April 26-29 in commemoration of the first Jamestown landing 400 years ago in Virginia Beach. White keynotes the open-

ing of the conference April 26 by joining with Bishop John & Pastor Anne Gimenez, of The Rock Church International, who are facilitating the conference.

White, the only female speaker, will be joined by many key Christian leaders including John Hagee, Rod Parsley, Kenneth Copeland, Pat and Gordon Robertson, as well as a many other Virginia Beach area churches with hopes of renewing a 400 year-old covenant with God for a new generation, and that righteousness would once again exalt a nation.

"To the Glory of God we will continue with the vision of our forefathers, declaring that Jesus Christ has birthed freedom to a nation and reminding future generations that ours is a generation that honored God by remembering the 400 year-old covenant with Him and the anniversary of our nation's birth," White said. "Proverbs 22:28 tells us 'remove not the ancient landmark, which our fathers have set.' And this is our mission to consecrate this time in history and this conference as a time to honor God and our forefathers who gave their lives so we can be free. These were men and women that by their faith overcame tremendous odds as forerunners to our great nation."

The conference comes right in the wake of a gag lifted on guides at the historic Jamestown, VA site, preventing them from describing much of the Christian influence at the settlement after confirming that records show the "propagation" of Christianity was, in fact, a major goal of the newcomers to the continent. (Consecration Conference, 2007)

I didn't have to pay for a hotel because I already had a

room available, so all I really had to cover was my food. At this time, I was pretty much on a shoe string budget, and I wasn't spending anything that I wasn't supposed to. Because I had been self-employed and I had done so well, the back taxes I owed were over fifteen thousand dollars. But I still decided I was going to go to this conference.

The first day of the conference came, and I had gotten there entirely too early. There was this area where you could get coffee, and I really like coffee, and it had a whole bunch of windows that allowed the sun to shine on me, and it felt so good. I walked through that area, and I saw an older lady sitting at a table by herself, Miss Reverend Stephanie. I can be a somewhat social person at times, so I thought I would go and talk to her. I walked over to the table and asked her if anyone was sitting there. She looked up at me and said, "You are". Over the next two days, we would talk, sit near each other in the conference, and I got to know her to some degree. We had a break later in that day, and she had her lunch. I broke out some ramen noodles I had brought. They didn't have a microwave, so I decided I would just eat them dry. She thought this was one of the funniest things she had ever seen. I didn't think anything about it because that was all I had at that moment, and it was okay to me.

The next night, we had a conversation about the prosperity of God (I remember I was eating ramen noodles). I asked her if she knew that God was the owner of the cattle on one thousand hills or if Solomon was so rich in the Bible that they would pile the silver up in hills outside of the kingdom because it was not worth counting anymore. God always has the ability to provide anyone's needs. I asked her if she knew that, if God needed to get money to her, he would cause a big diamond to come up from the ground so that you would trip over it? If we would just listen and do what he tells us to do, he could get everything we need. After getting very excited about this conversation, she looked up at me and said, "I think I am going to take you to eat somewhere. What would you like? My treat.", she told me. I told her I didn't have a preference, especially if I was not paying. She asked if I liked Olive Garden, and I answered of course, my wife was Italian. I loved pasta and a good salad, and I believe Olive Garden has some of the best. So we went and had a wonderful dinner full of great conversation about the things of God and what we thought about the conference.

The next day, we were back at the conference for another night. There was a speaker that came on that evening. I don't remember his name, but he asked for an offering. I remember feeling so compelled to give into the offering. I gave the only forty dollars I had on me. I was not sure how much we had in the account since my wife was usually the one that was responsible for the bank account. I remember being all excited about giving the offering, and I called my wife to let her know what I had done. I told her about how I gave to this speaker. She asked me if I had lost my mind. That was the last forty dollars we had in the account. She had bought some groceries, and knew I would get paid in a couple of days, so she was not worried about spending the money. So she asked me how in the world I was going to make it home. It was about a two hundred and forty mile drive, which at the time pretty much took a full tank to do. I told her I knew what God had told me do, and everything would be okay, even if I have to stand at a gas station and have a total stranger pay my bill for me. She let me know of her disbelief and told me I could figure out how to get home then, and that was the end of that conversation. They had about one more hour of the conference and then we would be finished for the night. I spent a little more time talking to Rev. Stephanie, and she let me know that she had to head back first thing in the morning because her time share had finished. She had been down for her vacation when she saw that there was a conference. She told me to take her wristband and give it to anyone I saw that may want to come to the conference the next day. I thought that was a great idea, so I gladly took it. I had gotten her contact information, promised we would stay in touch, and we went on our merry ways.

The next morning, I got up to do the last appraisal that I had in the area before I was to head home. I got to the inspection and went to the front door, but nobody answered. I knocked again in case I was a little early and someone did not hear me. I waited outside for several minutes, and there was still nothing. I called the number and still nothing. So finally after about ten minutes, I figured the home owner was a no show, so I was getting ready to leave when the lady answered the door. She was in her late forties to mid fifties, slender in nature, and had an elegant and classy appearance. As she opened the door, she looked quite puzzled. She asked if I could help her. I introduced myself and told her I was there for the inspection. She looked puzzled then said that she thought that was next week. I informed her that, per my file, I had the inspection set up for this week. She said that she was not expecting this, her house was not clean, and she would prefer for me to not do the inspection that day.

I informed her I would have to try to set up a new time and that someone else in my office would probably be the one that would complete it. She paused for a couple of minutes then said,

"I guess you can go ahead and do it today, but can you go ahead and start outside." This was fine as I preferred starting outside anyway. So, I thanked her and started my inspection on the outside and informed her it should take me about fifteen to thirty minutes to get the basic exterior inspection completed. She agreed and I did the exterior inspection. When I moved inside, she asked me how my weekend was going and what I had done. I told her that I had gone to a Christian conference. After a few minutes and while I was doing the inspection, she told me she was believing to build a school/hospital for kids that were in need. I agreed that God was able to help her get that done, no matter the cost.

Then the conversation shifted to the Consecration Conference and how I had a wonderful time but would be heading back home today. I told her that I had a wristband that a friend had given me, if she wanted to go the last day. She said that she had wanted to go but was not able to this weekend. She had a very puzzled look on her face for a few minutes. I continued to do the inspection and, after several minutes, she came to me and asked if we could pray. I said sure, this was very awkward to me, as I had not had many people do this to me before, especially at an inspection.

I agreed for her to pray, and she took me into her living room and got a prayer shawl. Until then, I had only seen some Jewish people with a prayer shawl, and I was starting to find this weird. She began to speak in tongues, and although I had grown up around it, I was still thinking that it was getting a little creepy. I also remember that while she was praying, I started thinking, man, she sure is gripping my hands hard. Nothing she said really bothered me, it just seemed so weird. So right about three-fourths of the way through her praying, she stopped and said,

"I don't mean to imply anything or to be rude, but I believe I am supposed to give you some money." I told her that she was not supposed to give me money for the inspection and that she had already paid the client. She said she knew that, but she was talking about giving ME money! She said she wanted to give me two hundred dollars, and I was shocked. I let her know that this could not affect the results of the inspection in any way. She laughed and informed me she didn't really need the inspection anyway. She asked me if a check was okay, and I told her yes, of course. After she started writing the check, I told her what had been going on. She said I now had enough money to get home and take my lovely wife out to dinner. But as I went to leave, it occurred to me that banks were not open on Sunday, and I would not be able to cash the check until to-morrow. I looked cautiously back to her and asked her if there was any way she could give me cash. She said if I could follow her to the ATM, she would be glad to get me some money. She did so, and I went on my merry way. I will never forget what she did for me that day.

A Lesson Learned

I will never forget the goal and vision this woman had. She was believing God for a large building so she could help kids. I do not know if this woman was rich or if that was the last money she had. But I have never have forgotten the grace and compassion she showed to a perfect stranger, in a time where I didn't know that I could go any lower in my life. When I remember, I still think of this women and pray that the seed she has sown prospers so that she may have the vision come to pass in her life that she believed God for. I still have hope that I will once again meet this woman!

Prayer

Lord, I ask that for all those that have shown your love, let their visions, dreams, hopes and aspirations affect them and the lives around them. Let them complete everything you have called them to do, and let them have all the provision they need because they have shown that they have a heart like the father. Father, if we don't have the right heart, show us, so we might change and forever be more like you!

CHAPTER 41

Losing Blood

A FEW MONTHS LATER, one of the next big things of that year happened. My son was diagnosed with Crohn's Disease or Ulcerative Colitis. Cameron was six years old, almost seven. He was really into inline speed skating at the time. I remember he was competing in the semi-regionals at the Star City Skate Center right off Hershberger Road. We started noticing a few of the comments that he was saying, how he would have to keep running to the bathroom and complaining that his stomach was hurting when he would go to the bathroom. We thought it was odd but figured he had too much cheese or something and was a little constipated. He was by far one of the fastest in his age groups when it came to skating.

We had never forced him to skate, but his coach Porky was extremely tough on Cameron because of his potential. He would always have Cameron compete with kids that were twice as big, old, and fast. He would ask Cameron why he was not beating them because they were all slower than him.

Cameron always rose to the challenge and, because of that, he ranked very high in most of the competitions. We were at the regionals, and Cameron was skating. I swear that boy would never run out of energy. Ever since he was small, he liked to go walking, running, swimming, riding bikes, and skateboarding. It never really mattered what he was doing, as long as he could go fast and use lots of energy. It seemed that he had an everlasting endurance, but this day he was complaining about running out of energy. He said that he was getting tired and felt like he could not breathe. He placed first in his class, and he was scheduled to go to regionals. We were almost positive he would have placed and went to nationals that year. Not that we had the money for it, but we were still going to help support our child in his dreams. But over the next few days, he kept complaining about being tired and cramping. This got my wife very concerned and so we agreed that he should go to the doctor. This is when we discovered that he had a severe case of Crohn's. They estimated that he was losing about one-fourth a cup of blood a day, and he was so tired because he had lost too much iron and was now completely anemic. They admitted him to the hospital where he would spend the next two weeks.

I remember how the whole family was there trying to be supportive because this was a very big deal. This was quite the ordeal, and I wondered what we were going to do. The doctors come in and told us that they think it might be beneficial to have twenty-five feet of his small intestines removed. My wife and I said they needed to come up with another option. The doctor came back several hours later the option of an experimental drug called Humera©.

They had to give him something called goofy juice, which was a drug to knock him out, so that they could get a tube through his nose and down his throat. They fed him directly with a drip formula to reduce strain on his stomach. Before they could do this, they had to give him several shots, and since they knew they were going to admit him, they gave him an IV in his hand.

I was trying to make light of the situation by acting like I was going to faint from the sight of blood. I remember being bothered for him, and kind of scared for him, but was being a jokester trying to keep everything light hearted by making jokes. I start joking near the ledge by the windows in the hospital like I was having a seizure. The next thing I remembered, I was on the floor with several nurses over my head. I had apparently blacked out. This had happened several years before when I had cut my finger while in the Navy. The nurses gave me a few minutes, helped me into a wheel chair, checked my vitals, and told me to drink some water. This really scared Cameron, which was the opposite of what I was trying to accomplish at the time.

They finished the IV, wheeled me and Cameron back to the room, and waited for the drugs to kick in. After they gave him the goofy juice, he began to relax and start laughing. One of the things that became the highlight of the room was making fun of me passing out and shaking like I had on the floor. So he would shake and then laugh. This went on for several minutes while he was playing video games in his hospital room. Then after about ten minutes, he started to lose his motor abilities and began to lose general physical functions. This really bothered him and made him very scared. But just a minute or two later, he was asleep. They went ahead and inserted the tube down his throat. This was to give him some of the nutrients and things that they needed to give him to get him better, although apparently some of them did not have the best taste.

Over the next two weeks, I would work during the day and then come to the hospital to sleep. We would listen to healing sermons, I would have my son listen to scripture nightly, and over the next two weeks he improved a great degree. The doctors were thrilled with the turnaround and were impressed by the change they had seen. The inflammation was so bad that he was not allowed to have any solid food for two weeks. He would remain on the drip for an additional two weeks after he got home with only soft foods until the inflammation would go away. Over the next weeks, we would become familiar with the process of in-home nurses and constant checkups. But after about a month, he was released by the doctors as being fully fit and able to return to school.

A Lesson Learned

Many times, a man, father, or husband has to put on a face that they are strong and unaffected by traumatic things. But I tell you, any man, woman, or child that has a gentle, loving, and compassionate heart like our father God is moved, especially when their child or others' children are affected. But I have learned that when you have different people yelling in your ear about how you are in an impossible situation, the best thing you can do is thank them but understand that they are not God! God's not done with this situation yet! They have not seen your Daddy in action!

Prayer

Daddy, Father, You are a great big God and you love me!
You love me, kids, family, employees, spouse, and because
of your love, grace, and mercy, I ask you into this situation.
I ask you to come and do mighty miracles, and I will give you
all the glory, all the praise and all the credit, in Jesus Name I
pray, Amen!

CHAPTER 42

A Job but No Money

OVER THE NEXT FEW months, the real estate market would begin to tank. I went from making about seventy thousand a year to about ten thousand a year almost overnight. My bills were almost five thousand dollars a month, and like almost everyone I lived paycheck to paycheck. I had been making very good money, but my bills were very high. I would spend the next six months using credit cards to pay some of my bills because I knew this was just a small dip and that I would get the work back soon and be able to catch up. I had done this before and had recovered so this was no big thing. But the market did not come back, and the company stopped giving us work because they personally needed the income. So we did what most anyone would do, we cut down on almost all the expenses that we thought we could at the time. We reduced our bills to about three thousand dollars a month. The problem was, I was the only one that was working at the time and was only making about one thousand per month. So each month I was going in debt about two thousand.

I was learning about believing God for things, so I wrote a check for four thousand dollars and put it in a little box that I had. I was believing "in faith" for enough money to pay things off, get ahead, and be a giver. But the thirty thousand dollars that I believed for never came. All my bills were getting behind and stress was pressing on the relationship with my wife. I was behind on everything. I remember telling my wife that I was going to tithe no matter what. She got very mad at me and told me if I did that they were going to turn the electric off and we would be without lights. There were little to no groceries in the house. I was not getting hardly any work, and I had applied to work at VDOT for an Imminent Domain and Right of Way Appraisal Position. I had been volunteering as much as I could at the church I was attending at the time. They did not have any paid positions, so I continued doing any work that I could. I was volunteering about twenty to forty hours a week believing God for a job that would cover my bills, which I was convinced was the VDOT job. I was very unqualified for this type of job, however. I had almost no knowledge about roadway construction, imminent domain, or condemnation procedures. I also had little to no actual experience, but I still believed God for it.

I was doing a lot of volunteering at the church, but what almost no one knew was that we didn't have hardly any food at the house. I surely didn't have money to go to Burger King©, McDonald's©, or any other fast food place around there. Many days, I got to church to work around noon and would be there sometimes until ten o'clock at night. I would have not eaten since about six most mornings, and that meal might have consisted of a couple of eggs and some toast. People like Joe Mays would ask me if I would like some lunch. At first, I would never tell them yes because I didn't have the money to pay for it. So one day, when Joe asked me if I would like something, I told him it was not really in my budget. He said, "I never asked you to pay for it, son. I asked if you wanted some lunch." I told him "Yes, Sir," and he asked me what I wanted and later came back with my meal. I ended up having several people do that: Carl, Lana, Brenda, Joe, Ken, Rocky, etc. I was there so much that the church offered me a temporary contractual job doing construction. The job lasted two weeks, and they gave me a little bit extra on the check.

My grandmother came to visit a few weeks later. She ended up spending several weeks with my mom. Her friend that had driven her there had some issues and needed to leave early. She flew back home leaving my grandmother at my mom's home. Her friend also left her dog with my grandmother. So my grandmother Ethel was essentially stranded in Virginia. She lived in Ferriday, Louisiana. She knew I was having some money issues so she told me that she was willing to pay me to take her home. It was fourteen hours one way to drive her home. She told me that she would give me five hundred dollars to drive her and would pay for all the gas and food. I agreed and when she decided to leave, I drove her. We stopped when she asked and walked the dog. We got up early that morning and with all the stops got her home about ten o'clock that night. It was a very long day on the road. This would be one of the last times I would see her before she would become pretty sick.

I had called Milton and Irma, who at this time lived in Atlanta, Georgia; they were the couple that had gotten me saved when I was six years old. It was only going to be a few hours from where I was. I talked to Milton and found out that Irma was not going to be around, but he would love to have me come by. So I agreed and dropped off my grandmother. I spent the day and night there then proceed to go home the next day. It was so nice to see them, as I had not seen them in several decades. At that particular moment, they were available for me to spend some time with them. We had not really spoken in several years prior, even though they were always considered to be part of the family. Yet still they opened their home to me, gave me a place to stay, and saved me the money that I would have had to spend most likely on a hotel, food, and travel. Their generosity was at a perfectly needed moment.

A Lesson Learned

Never under value a meal, cup of water, or something to eat or drink. Jesus said if you have even given a glass of water to the least of these, then you have done it to Him. I have been the least of these many times in my life. If you really haven't spent time with people in their home, you really for the most part, have no actual idea what they are really going through. I don't know who said this, but I have heard it said "I would rather give a bad man a break, then break a good man."

Prayer

God I ask you for wisdom and revelation to know who to help and how to help them. Let me be sensitive to your words, your love, and how to help others around me. Let me never judge a book by its cover, but only by the content of its character.

CHAPTER 43

Interview Gone Right

SEVERAL MONTHS LATER, WE were still in Heather-wood apartments. It had taken almost six months for me to get VDOT to do interviews. I remember being so nervous during the interview board. They asked me about road construction, reading plans, Eminent Domain and Condemnation, and Right of Way; I had read about them, but they had no real bearing on any of the type of work I had done at the time. I didn't have any of that kind of experience, but I had read plans doing normal construction with Luke, and I had done so much volunteering with several different people that many people had written me letters of recommendation. It didn't hurt that I had Veteran preference status either.

So after multiple interviews, I was offered a job. The job was starting at thirty-three thousand a year. While I was there, I had two mentors, Becky, my direct supervisor, and Don. Becky was my main mentor, but she seemed to be kind of quiet, and I didn't always seem to understand her or jive with her. I think it was just a personality thing, but she was an excellent teacher and mentor. I remember that many times she would let me do something completely wrong. She would then ask me all these questions, tell me how my logic was right, but then she would bring up some methodology I had not paid attention to and then would start to explain all the different reasons of how I was wrong. She would tell me to go work the problem out again. I would do it, but then I would have still forgotten something else. It seemed like she did this every day.

When I got tired of feeling beat up, I would go and ask Don questions. He was her husband and was a great guy. He taught me more things about me, life, grace, love, and business than anyone person I had known at this point in life. Every day he would allow me to ask him questions about methodologies, appraisals, and even life, sometimes for hours. He was probably the most practical, and patient man I had ever met. I contribute much of my success to some very simple things he taught me.

I would type my reports up, and Becky would get that red pen of hers out and she would start correcting my work. I would want to stand over her shoulder and see what I was getting wrong like a school kid in trouble. But she would tell me to go sit down and work on other things and she would give it to me when she was done. I would reluctantly do so and then about two hours later or sometimes even the next day, she would give me my work back. I swear it looked like someone had been over the top of my paper, stabbing them, like it was a bleeding victim. It would have so many different red marks all over it. I would then do all the corrections I thought I was supposed to do. She would look at it again, and I swear it would look just as bad as the first time. This would continue basically every day for the next six months. I would work on something, she would correct it, I would talk to her, talk to Don to get clarification, and I would do it all over again. I was making thirty-three thousand a year and I had three to four thousand in bills a month. I was still losing money, so I started trying to do side appraisal jobs. I was doing several small business ventures with Charles as well. I was trying to make that forty thousand that I was still believing God for. I started doing so many other things while I was at work, I was fired! I was doing too many other things at my work that was not from that work. I was doing so because I was still about twenty thousand short a year on income from what I owed, even with this job, because I owed about twenty thousand in back taxes from where I had gotten so far behind. I did not respect that job like I should have and because of it, I lost it. This, however, would later give me the motivation I needed to do several other things.

A Lesson Learned

The bible says, "He who is faithful in a little is also faithful in much." I was not being faithful at the time.

> *Matthew 25:29: To those who use well what they are given, even more will be given, and they will have an abundance. But from those who do nothing, even what little they have will be taken away. (NLT)*

Prayer

Lord, teach us how to use the things that you have given to us well. Let us value people, money, relationships, and friendships, so that we can value and cherish them to know that they are gifts of God. As we do this, I thank you that you will add more to me, teach me more, and help me grow.

CHAPTER 44

No Job and No Money

I NOW HAD NO job and even less money. I was about three months behind on my car payment. The company called me to let me know that if I didn't pay them something, they were going to send someone that week to repossess my car. At the time, I had twenty-one dollars and ninety-seven cents in my account. I remember that amount for some reason even to this day. I was speaking with the representative, and my wife was listening and letting me know all the different options that we had available to try and resolve this. I told her that I didn't have the money to catch the car payment up at the moment. She told me that they had a deferment program, but she needed me to give her twenty-five dollars. The problem was that twenty-one dollars and ninety-seven cents was still several dollars short. I told her that I didn't have it in the account that day, so she wanted a post-dated check for the next day. I told her that would be fine. I figured that I would be able to borrow enough money from someone for gas and the twenty-five dollars for this deferment program that this woman was telling me about.

So while I was on the phone with her, she was in my account asking me a bunch of questions. By now we had been on the phone for over a half hour. She got kicked out of the program that she was working in, the one with all our account information. I heard a pause on the other end of the line. I asked her if anything was wrong, and she said something weird happened. We were like, what happened? She said that either someone had kicked her out of the system or someone logged into our account. We asked her why someone would have logged in our account. She said she was not sure, so she asked us to hold on for a little bit. We agreed as it seemed that she was already doing us a favor by doing the deferment on our account. She came back just a minute later and said, "That is really weird." The suspense at this point was very intense. We were like, "What!?" And she said, "Did you all just make a deposit?" We said no, and she asked if we were sure, and we said we were sure, knowing that we had no money in the account. It occurred to me to ask her if she could tell me who had made the deposit into the account. She said it was a Mr. Bob and Mr. Tim (names have been changed), which were Shi's uncles whom had been together for over twenty years. "They just caught your account up to date."

Just a couple of days later, a minister called from this little Baptist church down the road. He said that he had spoken with someone I knew at work, and they had requested that he come by our house to speak with us and help us out. We agreed, and he came by the house one evening. I was speaking with him, and he was listening to what we were going through. I had told him that God had supplied us with everything we needed, even though I did not like how much pressure we were constantly under due to how much we were still lacking. He told me,

"You just can't expect God to always pay your bills or send someone to pay your bills," as he was writing us a check. I thought this was really humorous since I believed God for everything and God had sent a man I didn't know to pay a bill that he was telling me I can't believe God to pay. I always found so much humor in that. He also informed me that he had Crohn's Disease and that it was horrible and that my son was going to have to live with it his whole life. I told him that I knew God was a healer and that my son would not have to live with this his whole life. This has been my confession and stance ever since the doctors said it was incurable.

Coming from our previous lifestyle, this was quite the shock. Going from having literally anything we wanted to having to pick what was the most economical just to keep us full. I went to my church and told them I was really having some problems. I didn't really tell them the extent of the problems, but I said I was wondering if they could possibly help with some groceries. They told me that they didn't really have the funds for it and were not able to help at the time. I was kind of miffed at the moment, but I had to remind myself that God is my source and not a church or people. I had discussed some of this with Don and Terry who were a couple of guys at my work. I had let them know that if they knew of anyone or organization doing that type of help to let me know. I was willing to work and do other things but just needed a little extra help to get some groceries. They told me they understood and looked into some stuff, but I think it was even a few weeks before he ever said anything back to me.

The food in the house was becoming basically non-existent. I remember looking in the pantry and having only a six pack of ramen left one day. I remember thinking, what are we going to do, there still was not enough money to pay the bills, we had just had someone pay our car and electricity. I should at least be able to bring some food into the house. Terry from VDOT got in touch with someone at Angel Food, which was a local Christian food bank, and gave me a box of food. It had things like hamburger helper, peanut butter and jelly, some bread, but no meat. I was so thrilled, because now Cameron could at least have some things he was familiar with. I had not even told my parents how bad I was struggling. I just didn't want to hear another lecture from family, friends, or colleagues on how I screwed up or didn't plan. So instead I just didn't say anything. I knew I had messed up a lot of stuff, so I was doing everything I could to learn things about money, God, tithe, finances, business, life, and marriage. So for the first time in my life, I stopped running from God but toward God! I stopped "Running from Miracles" and decided "It's Time to Come Home".

A Lesson Learned

Probably one of the most important lessons I ever learned, was from a comment a minster by the name of Joyce Meyers said, "Sometimes you don't get to know God, till God is all you got!" This is a simple statement but very profound.

Prayer

God, I ask for a fresh realization that only you are my source! Not my friends, family, job, kids, life, work, spouse, etc. Only you can help me, but if I have you, I've got everything I need.

CHAPTER 45

A Shift

DON HAD BEEN SUPER gracious to me at VDOT, teaching me life skills. He had also talked to me about a lot of different business things from the business he had started. He gave me some personal contacts and also told me some basic things to grow a business. At the time, I was with a group called the Roanoke REIA that Charles had originally started. He had planned an event and had people coming, but one of the speakers cancelled on him last minute. He asked me to step in as a speaker. For that particular conference, he was charging about three thousand dollars for a three day event. Two of the big topics were negotiations and creative financing. He had brought in several other speakers at the time that were all pretty much in either marketing or the real estate industry.

I had asked my parents to start an appraisal business with me about a year prior to this, but they were very reluctant at the time. I decided then that I was going to start a business on my own. I thought, what is the worst that could happen, I was already completely broke. In the last six months, I had realized we had a really bad financial problem; so we got out of our apartment, cut every expense, and moved back in with my wife's mom in downtown Roanoke, VA. This was something that I really did not like doing. I was very independent, and it had not been very good for our marriage when we had lived with her in the past. She was forced to get a real job. I was told just as we were moving out of the apartment that she didn't want to be married to me anymore. She replied,

"I wanted you saved enough to not run around on me, but I didn't want you this saved". This was a testing moment of my faith, and in that moment, it showed as I began to throw things across the house, cussed up a storm, and proceeded to go down to the store, and buy two packs of cigarettes and a six pack. I had not done this in years, but I had quit them all for the wrong reasons. So over the next month, I moved back in with her mom, but most of the time I was to sleep at the back bedroom of the house, which was really more of an enclosed porch. We also became legally separated for the second time in our marriage. This got everything started toward a divorce and allowed her to start getting benefits from the state, since I couldn't even provide food for the table.

A Lesson Learned

We do so many things in life for all the wrong reasons. So when we get to the end of the day, we don't have any strength or stamina, because we have no real foundation on why we started a particular thing. New diet, removing of addictions, cussing, drinking, sex, pornography, gossiping, etc. If you do them for the wrong reason, even if they are a great thing, lots of time you will have no perseverance when trouble or situations come. But yet even still, God was in the middle!

Prayer

God, help me make you the center of why I do things, things that are lasting, consistent, good and constant. Teach me to see you in every part of my life, to see you at the bottom and to see you at the top. Because without you, I would not have another breath to see either.

CHAPTER 46

The Proposal

I HAD DEVISED A plan to start a business. I had been trying to learn everything I could about it for about a year or so because the market was getting really bad. I figured I could do at least as bad as the other guy. So I came up with a proposal with investors, that if they let me borrow ten thousand dollars, then they would get five percent of the profit of the company and fifty dollars from every appraisal until the loan was paid back. But if it busted, then they didn't get anything back and I don't owe a dime to anyone. This was a pretty bold proposal I thought, but right after the meeting, a guy walked up to me and asked,

"Cash, Check, or Charge?" I was absolutely dumb founded. I told him that I needed forty-eight hours to respond. He agreed, and I left for the day. I went to my parents later that day and told them I wanted to start the company. It would take about five thousand dollars to get it off the ground, but I needed an answer in about twenty-four hours. My mom asked me a few questions, we set some basic perimeters of what the company was going to look like, and we got started. My mom was on unemployment at the time, and she knew how to sign up some of the clients, so she showed me how to do that. I was already familiar with the appraisal software and appraisals, so that was the easy part. We started signing up clients. Don was still always available for me to call and ask any question, and man I was so happy he was. I had gotten a little website up, was doing some basic work for a few clients, and had expanded our area as much as we could.

Around the June to July time frame, my wife was sure that she wanted a divorce to such a point that we were not even really talking, but I still lived in the same house. I was in the back enclosed porch, and she had started talking to a guy at her work. He was a charmer, and they worked together, and he had all the right stuff to say. Especially on how bad of a husband I was, how I didn't really love her, and all the fun stuff that goes with it. Based on what I had done, how could I blame her, right? But one night, she had told me that she was going to spend the night with one of her friends. I didn't believe her, so later that night I decided to go swing by where she said she was going. When I arrived at the apartment, no one was there. She was not answering her phone, so I went by another one of her friend's house, and she was not there either. So I realized she was at this guy's house, the new boyfriend. I saw that it was pretty much over, and I decided that I was going to a bar and have a drink.

I swung by Mango's, which is on Smith Mountain Lake. I went, sat down, and got a drink. This girl that was in front of me turned around and asked me if I was having fun yet. This was very funny to me because that was always one of my lines as an ice breaker to people. Now this girl that I have never met was saying the same thing to me. I thought it to be quite ironic. I looked at her and replied,

"I'm having a blast, how 'bout you?" Me and this girl, Amanda, began to talk and exchange information. After the bar closed, we went to Denny's where we had coffee and talked for several more hours. Our situations were very similar; she too was separated and had a son. We connected over our pain. About two weeks later, my wife was in the bath, and I went in there and asked her if we were working things out or not. I just needed a final answer! She hemmed and hawed and still did not really have a response. I looked at her and told her, well, I am going on a date then! She started to cuss and yell, and I left for my date.

I didn't have any money, so I invited her to do something that wouldn't cost me anything. I invited her to the Blue Ridge Parkway. I figured it would be fun, quiet, and kind of romantic, but it was mostly so we could be alone. We headed down to the spot near the dam that was right there, and we began to walk down the hill. It was about a mile walk, and it was pretty steep. She, of course, did not have on proper shoes, so she had to hold my hand to be steady. This was not my first time in the rodeo. We talked and I asked questions, and more questions, and more questions. I was making sure this girl was not crazy. We had all sorts of conversation and then we walked back to the top, and had some very intense kissing. We were almost inseparable from that point on.

That November, I got a call from a lady that was having an eminent domain issue. I called Don, and I ended up doing my first consulting job. We charged her about four hundred dollars for about six hours of work, but she got an additional ten thousand from the state. She was happy, and I was thrilled. I didn't get to use the money for Christmas, but at least I could keep my car one more month. We had started the company in May of 2008, but it was now December, and money was still so very tight. I made so little that year, and I told everyone I was not able to do Christmas for anyone, not even my son Cameron. So Christmas rolled around, and I had tried to make a few things that I already had, but I just didn't have anything. My sister was so moved that she bought the presents and put my name on them so that I would have something to give people so I would not be embarrassed.

Several of the gifts were very meaningful to people, and they asked me where I got it, and I would just tell them what my sister had done. I remember having to excuse myself several times. I would go out to the back and just sob! This was the bottom; almost every day, I would have to force myself to get up and live, just one more day! That year, the company grossed about twenty-two thousand dollars. This was between me and my dad working. That year, between me waiting tables at night and appraisals, I had a gross income of thirteen thousand for the entire year. I would get up every morning and be at work by nine o'clock and would work to three o'clock that afternoon and then go wait tables. But between nine and three, we didn't have work, so I would go and try to make calls, sign up clients, get better software, look at what we needed, and go to other meetings to see if there were things I could learn about marketing. This became my daily routine. Between being broke, having a son who didn't want to talk to me, and being back living with my parents, things were not fun. This was a year of tears!

By the following May, which was the one-year anniversary of the business, work had started picking up some. We changed our areas around so that now we were only covering local areas such as Lynchburg, Roanoke, and New River Valley (Tri-Cities). This was about a forty-five mile radius from the office. This was no distance compared to what we had been used to covering. The company made about fifty-eight thousand that year, which was substantial growth to the year before. The company would also be debt free within the eighteen months after we started it.

A Lesson Learned

Everyone has something to offer, the question is not if something has worth, but what is the worth and can you see it. I started to learn how to value business, ideas, relationships, myself, and also, you have to learn what to give up on. I think for me this was one of the hardest things I ever did, was to simply stop, to quit, to give up! Because before you can start something new, you have to give up on something that is dead! Because I have spent my entire life, believing in an all-powerful, all restorative, all consuming, all revealing God. I have not learned that there are many people that don't want any part of something being restored, fixed, refreshed and/or being renewed, and this is when you need to learn, you must, just simply walk away!

Prayer

Show me the value of both my good and negative characteristics, my good and bad flaws; teach me to be patient and kind but yet with understanding. Not only to myself but with others around me. Show me how to preserve in every situation, yet learn to realize I am not God and I cannot nor will I ever force anyone to change.

CHAPTER 47

Reuniting with a Friend

I HAD STILL KEPT in touch with Rev. Stephanie over the last two years, even though we had not seen each other for some time. It was still her tradition to go down to Virginia Beach, Virginia for her timeshare vacation. One particular day, she gave me a call and said that she had been walking on the boardwalk. Her knees were not the best and had begun to lock up. The problem was she had walked about a mile from the hotel and had left her credit card and ID back in the room. This meant no money, no cab, and still having to try and get back. She called me, and very rarely do I not pick up the phone, so I answered and she told me she needed some help.

She let me know what she has done, and I began to talk to her about the healing power of God, how God is always faithful, and that if she would just believe God for one more step, then she could make it back to the hotel. I spent the next forty-five minutes talking to her about the strength and faithfulness of God and how He has never failed us when we believe in him. She would walk that day by faith that entire mile and get back to her hotel room. We still joke today about her calling me. She told me she could have called anyone, but she called me because I wouldn't give her "none of that fluff"; I would only say what the Word says, no matter if she wanted to hear it or not.

A Lesson Learned

I have had a lot of people that have loved the "no fluff" me! But I have also been hated for the same thing! You are not made for every environment nor for every person. But one thing I didn't learn until writing this book is that she had no way back, "No ID, No Card". I figured she just needed some motivation. But I have learned helping someone does not mean you do it for them, it means that you assist them in understanding the tools they need to finish the task in front of them.

Prayer

Teach me to speak the truth, both in season and out of season. In other words, even if it doesn't make me popular, even when people are hurting, help me not to be mean or malicious but compassionate, understanding, and firm on the promises of God. To never falter, make allowances for being the victim, and own every decision I make in my life so I can live a life of victory and abundance in every area.

CHAPTER 48

The Power of Value

THE DAY THAT I was in the conference with Charles was the same day they had been talking about keywords. I had been doing appraisals for years and realized there was a direct separation in people's minds between appraisals (valuing things) and everything else. This almost became an obsession of mine. So much so that, no matter where I went, I would talk about it. One day I was at an appraisal, and I met the home owner, Charnika. We spent a little time together, and we noticed that we had some similarities in background, beliefs, and church perspectives. I spent some time talking with her and let her know that I would like to do a seminar. She spoke with her Pastor, and he allowed me to come do my first seminar. Every person that helped me with graphics, audio, video, posters, and advertising were people I had worked with in the Church or Ministry I had been in. "The Power of Value" was the name of the event, and we had already pre-sold video and audio recordings. But about half way through it, the slide on the computer messed up. But yet, overall, everything went really well.

In 2010, the company would do about seventy-eight thousand dollars in gross. I was beginning to be more and more involved in the church and with Amanda. There is a clause in Virginia that if you live with someone for more than seven years, they will legally declare you married. Things were starting to get serious, but after the last marriage, my statement was, "There is a greater chance that Virginia will declare us as married then you will get me to say 'I Do' again".

This was my stance, thought process, and pretty much what I was going to stick to about the whole concept of marriage. We had moved in together, which was very much frowned upon by several people in the church. I understood why, but due to all the pain and resentment, I would rather have people hate me and live in sin than for it to be like anything like what I left in my last marriage. She felt the same way because of her ex-husband. He had drank too much for many years, had incurred thousands of dollars in medical bills, (some of the reasons for the bankruptcy), and had a temper problem at the time. So just because we were seeing each other, this was a major problem. One particular occasion, he came down to her work and threatened to fight me.

Amanda and I were both legally separated and spent that year getting divorced, filing bankruptcy, getting kicked out of the trailer complex, and having to move because my son was not allowed to stay the night with us. They told Amanda she had thirty days to have the trailer out of the trailer park or to stop seeing me! She came to me and asked me what she was going to do. I told her I didn't know and asked her if she wanted me to leave and not come back? She told me no, that she had wanted me to stay. I had already spoken to my sister who was going to be nice enough to loan me three thousand dollars for moving expenses. The next two weeks getting everything moved seemed to be pure hell, but we got it done.

They downsized her job as a retail manager about three months later, and then she got laid off. She had been making about thirty-five thousand a year, which to us was really good money. Really, her job was the only reason we got to do anything. Her ex-husband refused to give her child support or keep a job. I was fifteen thousand dollars behind on back taxes, three thousand behind on child support, but I was finally breaking even. Now Amanda didn't have a job, and there was nothing I could do about any of it.

A Lesson Learned

Most of the time when you are trying to do something new, different, unique, or out of the norm, it is messy, sloppy, looks bad, unpopular, and most of the time is not the right way to do it. This book is full of my mistakes, sins, downfalls, and problems. I make no apologies for my mistakes, because I heard it said ,"I never made a mistake, but I have done a lot of things in life that have turned out to be a mistake." But many people never do anything in life out of fear of making a mistake. But if you are doing anything, you can't avoid making a mistake. So I have learned that if you are going to fail, fail forward.

Prayer

Let me do something I have never done, so if I do something and it turns out to be a mistake, at least I was doing something different. So God, give me the grace and wisdom to do things the right way. If things are done the wrong way, help me correct them, help me learn from them, and teach me your ways.

CHAPTER 49

Blood is Thicker than Water, But Love is Thicker than Blood

ONE THING ABOUT MY family is once you are family, you are always family. I think this would be one of the hardest Thanksgivings we would have. Shi, my newly divorced ex-wife, her new son, her mom, my son, and Amanda, all in the same home for Thanksgiving. We all managed to be cordial, but you could cut the tension with a knife this entire year. This was not something that I was okay with, but it was my parents' house and my parents' rules. Family was family, no matter the title or marriage status. This was one of the hardest and most awkward years for family events. But it has been said that blood is thicker than water, but I have learned that love is thicker than blood.

My parents loved the other side of the family I had started with and showed me and her the unconditional love that we should always have toward one another, even when we don't know how to. It doesn't matter how awkward the situation or uncomfortable you are; they are family no matter what they have done. You can love people and set proper boundaries. With enough time, we could go into the same house, joke, and have a good time, sometimes even enjoying each other's company and characteristics. Sometimes the miracle is just being okay with everything that didn't work out and being okay with bad choices you or other people made. My mom always made a comment that if people knew better, they would do better. That is not always true, but sometimes we make choices that are not always the best, but we can learn to be okay with the mistakes we make!

A Lesson Learned

To all those that have blended families, blood is thicker than water, and love is thicker than blood. This is the fabric that Jesus Christ went to the cross on, and this is why he died, not just for his chosen people, but for all that would believe in him! Are we not a little "blended" in the world?

Prayer

Help me see people for who they are and who you want them to be without anger, offence, or bad perspectives. Show me how to love like you do, teach me to walk the way you do!

Married: Not Happening

ABOUT THIS TIME, AMANDA and I had been together for about two years, and our pastor came up to us and asked us about when we were going to get married. I looked at him and told him it wasn't happening. This was a pure and simple philosophy for me; marriage equals problems, and I don't need any more problems in my life. Amanda was sweet, good-looking, kind, gentle, forgiving, frugal, a good worker, well educated, soft spoken, intelligent, fun to be around, energetic, and compassionate. But she had been married to an irresponsible drunk that was manipulative and had a mother that thought she was perfect. Some of these traits had come into her lifestyle, and it was causing some major problems.

After about six more months, our Pastor came to me again and asked about us doing marriage counseling. I agreed but was very reluctant and against the whole topic. My belief is that many are in love with the thought of marriage, but when it actually comes down to it, they love the idea more than the process it takes to have one. We went to counseling being very against it, but I was assured that this marriage would be different. I had still not proposed! Actually, I refused to ask because I wanted someone that actually wanted me, someone that was willing to ask! This was very against Amanda's way of doing it, and I was okay with us just not ever being married. We continued to go to counseling where I was assured that Amanda, Pastor, and my friends would be with me through the entire process. I would have someone to be there to help me, and us to make sure everything worked out the way it was supposed to. We continued to go through the pre premarital counseling for the next six months. She actually proposed to me one night, jokingly with a little plastic ring she had gotten from a gum drop machine. She had fulfilled the requirement, even though she detested it the entire time.

A Lesson Learned

Most marriages never have a chance because they never spend any time to ask questions. They never get to know each other, their problems, sins, attitudes, etc., and the marriage really never has a chance. But even when you do know these things, it does not prevent the marriage from having problems. The only thing that will truly help the marriage to be successful is selflessness and Christ being the center of every decision.

Prayer

Show me my ways Lord; show me my real intentions: the good, the bad, and the ugly. Show me what I need to be working on so that my spouse will want to be married to me! Show me where I am not taking responsibility, blaming, accusing, not loving, not listening, or not following! As You show me these things, help me, my marriage, and relationships! I thank You and love You for all that You have done!

CHAPTER 51

The Engagement

WE HAD DECIDED THAT we were going to get married, but I still had not proposed and she was pretty sure that I was not going to. We had gone down to a Tanger Outlet Mall, which was several hours from Roanoke. We had previously looked at several rings locally, but I had not seen anything that really caught my eye. She had worked in fine jewelry for years, so I was very nervous– no, terrified– about getting her a ring. Over the next few months, I would almost become a gemologist after all the studying of the different types of rings, cuts, ratings, certifications, and where they came from. The one I was going to get was going to be perfect. Only one little tiny problem, though; I really didn't have the money for a nice ring. I had applied for a Kay's Credit Card, and they had approved me. There was no way I was just picking it out all by myself, so she would go into the stores, and she would look at specific rings.

At Tanger, we had narrowed the selection down to three rings. I then told her to leave the store and go shopping somewhere else. I deliberated for a little while, changing out the side bands to make it a little more custom than what she was expecting. Two of the first sets were more classic with the adjoining engagement bands, but the one I would settle on was an emerald cut with two diamond side bands with etched engravings on the side, much like some of the nicer rings I had looked at. I spent the next little while purchasing the ring and getting everything set up. I had gone way over the budget, but she didn't know it, and there was no way she was going to get to see the ring.

We had begun to make plans for our wedding, which we figured would be on Memorial Day, which would fall on May twenty-sixth of the next year, 2012. We had decided that after we got married, we were going to go on a family vacation for our honeymoon. I had never been on an actual vacation. I was a workaholic, and it never seemed to be in the budget in my previous marriage, even though I was making much more money. I had paid for everyone else to go on one, I just had never seemed to find the time to go on one myself. Amanda had really wanted to have a honeymoon after we got married, but I told her that I had never been on a vacation with my son, so I would be willing to do some kind of honeymoon or something after, but my son was going to get to do something with me first!

This was not something she was okay with, but she reluctantly agreed. However, we did decide to try to do a little get away first, like a long weekend. It was February 2012, and it was right before Valentine's Day. She was going to pay for the trip, and it was going to be a long weekend where we could spend some time together. This was something that was much needed at the time. Her ex-husband had given us a box of Pot of Gold, by Hershey's® chocolates, and before we left, I had carefully taken a razor, cut open the box, and put the ring in center of it . We had gotten some wine and snacks, and we hit the road. I had placed the chocolate box behind my seat. It was the funniest thing because Amanda didn't typically like sweets that much, but she wanted to eat that box ten times in that five hour drive. I would try to stop at stores, restaurants, or anything to get her off that box of chocolates. Of course, I was trying to do it all casual so it saves up for the perfect time. So we made it to the beach, and we had gotten an ocean-front hotel looking over the water with a hot tub in the room. We got there a little late, so we enjoyed the view and went to bed. The next morning, we ate some eggs for breakfast and took a walk on the beach. Surprisingly, it was only a little cold considering it was February. As we were doing all the window shopping that she enjoys, I bought her some flowers.

It was in the afternoon, and we had taken a nap. I put the chocolates in the mini fridge with the wine. We woke up from our nap and now I felt that it was the perfect time. I asked her if she would like some wine and the chocolates now. She replied, "Nope, I'm good, but thank you baby!" This was the re-sponse I was not wanting. So she wanted to go hit some more stores up, and after a few hours, we came back, and it was about three o'clock in the afternoon. She was a little readier for a snack, so she went and got the chocolates and was sitting on the bed about to open them. I was frantically in my mind trying to figure out, how do I work this in! What do I say now? How do I say it? What if I don't do it right? All these thoughts were running through my head, so I acted like something was on the floor beside the bed where she was sitting and as she opened the sealed box. I looked up, took the ring, and asked her to marry me. She had asked me, and I had said yes, but now I wanted to know would she say yes. She did!

A Lesson Learned

If you are a man trying to propose to your woman, you pulled it off, and she liked it? Good God, that is a Miracle!

Prayer

I ask for room in my heart and attitude to do something I don't want to do to. I pray I would have a miracle moment that could last through the worst of times and the best. The worlds, stars, and all the words perfectly align so that we can have those precious moments, but even if it goes all wrong, let me spend every day laughing about it!

CHAPTER 52

Give More

I HAD BEEN A giver and tither for several years at this point, but in 2012, God had really challenged me to give even more. I remember being challenged to give the tithe like I had been doing, give as I believe God was leading me, and then to give an additional five percent on top of the ten percent. It still seemed like I owed everyone and their brother. I still owed ten thousand on taxes that I had a payment plan on, we had to get another car that year, and I had borrowed five thousand for a SUV that we got at an auction. So, an additional five percent was really hard on my budget. But it seemed like every month the money came in. This would happen for the next twelve months.

At the end of that, God challenged some thinking that I had. I had owed all these people, and I was making payments, but God challenged me to give from a place of not owing anyone. I was challenged to give from place of surplus instead of giving from a place of debt. I would take the same percentages that I was giving, and over the next twenty-four months, I would double it to pay off debts. In just under twenty-four months, I would pay off our SUV, my taxes, credit cards, and a student loan I had had for the previous ten years.

You're about to see some of the blessings that took place over the next few years because of me listening to what God had told me to do! When I had started doing some of this, Amanda thought it was kind of a waste. The next segment is written by Amanda, and you will really get to see all that God was doing. Even though she thought that we should use the money elsewhere, she saw that when you do it God's way, his goodness can never be matched.

SHAWN E. DECKER

A Lesson Learned

If you have never been free from debt, realize you can be! My company as well as our ministry is one hundred percent debt free! I currently have some personal debt, but I am still believing God to be free from that! I am not against debt; I am against what I see it do to people, their dreams, hopes, time, and relationships! I am against watching debt destroy all of them.

Prayer

Thank you for teaching me to live prosperously and humbly while living in abundance. I pray that I would put your word, works, and ways first. As I do these, I thank you for working in my life! Thank you for causing additional resources to come in, and I will be diligent to take them and free myself from this shackle. Let me never fall in love with the supply but with the supplier.

· 231 ·

CHAPTER 53

Amanda's Journey of Faith through Work

WHEN I MET SHAWN, I had been attending church pretty regularly, and they had even helped me financially when my first husband was hospitalized. I had started to know God better, but the God that Shawn knew and talked about was something foreign to me. We would each go to church on Wednesday night, me to a bible study and him to "regular" service. He would come back talking about healing lines and people "falling down in the spirit." I had never experienced anything like this, and I was curious. I never expected his church to allow us to attend together since we were living together at the time, but the Pastor told Shawn to bring me. That was when I started to learn about faith.

Not long after starting to attend church together was when I lost my job after ten years. During much of those ten years, I had tried to find other work but had not been successful. I had felt trapped. As much as losing that job scared me, I was also excited about the new opportunity. I thought I had a job lined up to start directly after my end date, but this was during the recession and auto crisis and the job was with a domestic car dealer. So, that job fell through, but I had hope that another would come along. I did mention, it was in the heart of the recession in 2009, right? Jobs were hard to find, and I found that I did not really know how to look for one the right way. At a job fair after my lay off, I ran into a classmate from high school who was now working for a federal grant that assisted dislocated workers. He encouraged me to come enroll in his program, and I did so. The program did not really help me much since I already had a bachelor's degree. There were not many trainings that they could pay for.

I spent nine months on unemployment, using up almost all of my 401K that I had been saving for the previous ten years. During those nine months, I spent a lot of time with God, praying and listening to every sermon on the TV or on CD that Shawn gave me, and he had a lot of them. I began to learn how to speak in faith, stand on God's promises of prosperity, and that God had a good plan for me. At one point, I had to choose between paying my tithe and buying groceries. I walked up front and put my tithe into the bucket; when I got back to my seat, the usher came and handed me an envelope. In the envelope was three hundred dollars, more than enough to get groceries. This was the first time I saw God provide all my needs after truly believing that He was my source. Others would also give little amounts to help out over those hard months. This was extremely encouraging to my faith at the time. Something I would not find out for seven more years was that it was Shawn who gave the money anonymously.

God had told him to do it that way so that my faith would be fed, and had I not been part of a conversation where he would tell someone what he had done, I'm not sure if he would have ever told me.

My unemployment extension was running out as well as the 401K, and I really needed a job. I was believing God for a job that would allow me to help others and that would not be back in retail again. After ten years, I did not want to go back to the nights, weekends, and all holidays. This was the work that had kept me from spending time with my son all those years. However, it seemed that the only responses I was getting from my applications and resumes were from retail. My friend with the grant told me that they were going to be adding another position doing what he did if I was interested. Was I! Finding a job had become one of the hardest things I had done, and this job was helping people. When it opened up, I applied. I, of course, was required to apply for multiple jobs each week for unemployment, so I had also applied with a furniture rental company that was close to home. I got both interviews, and they seemed to go well.

The furniture company was decent pay making about thirty-six thousand a year. It was close to home, but it was long hours, six days week and was not what I was believing for! They did not offer me the job, but implied it was mine if I wanted it; I had to let them know within two days. Turning down a job would mean losing my unemployment benefits, but letting them know if I was interested or not kept me safe. The other job seemed perfect but was lower pay, only being about twenty-six thousand a year. Additionally, my ex-husband had pretty much refused to pay any child support or help with the bills. There were many trips into town amongst all the drama, fights, and cops being called. I had been in the process of taking him to court several times, but it was just one type of bureaucracy after another. Several of the other social workers had told me that I could pretty much expect there was nothing I could do and to not expect anything. I remember at first being very angry about this, but Shawn would always assure me that God is faithful and that He would make sure my needs were met. I remembered learning to rely on God for this without being bitter and upset.

I struggled with what to do. I could take the good pay that I needed or I could wait for what I had believed God for. He told me the other job would be mine! It did not make logical sense to turn down a given. One afternoon, Shawn and I went to lunch, and I was telling him about the struggle I was having about losing the benefits and how I wasn't getting the response from other people that I was expecting. In the middle of my tears during a lunch that day, he looked at me plain as day and said,

"If you believe that the job is yours, that God gave you the job, then it is yours". So after many tears and prayers, I turned the job down. Then I found out just a couple of days later that the other job was offered to someone else who was more qualified. I graciously thanked them for the interview, but I was confused; that was my job! I remember being very disappointed because it had not gone the way that I thought it should go. Shawn very sternly assured me to stay in faith. I kept working on my confession and staying positive, and a few weeks later, I saw that the same job was listed as open again. I emailed the hiring manager to let her know that I had

• 235 •

seen the posting and that I was still interested. Later that day, my phone rang, and she asked me to come in for another interview, this time with her supervisor. The other person who was more qualified had not made it through a whole day, and since I had already been through one interview and the background check, I was offered the job! God had once again come through in response to my faith.

That job was a blessing in many ways, but as you would remember, it was significantly less in pay than what I needed by about ten thousand dollars. They took a chance on me and trained me in a field that I knew nothing about. The learning curve was steep, but I loved it and attended every training they offered and got every certification I could. The pay was not good and the benefits for dependents were horrible, but I was able to keep my son covered through subsidized insurance. One of the other concerns about this job was that it was grant funded, so it seemed like every year, you were not sure that the grant would be renewed and you would still have a job. Shawn always encouraged me that if God could give me the job, he could help me keep the job. After the first year, I had received a raise. It was about two thousand for the first year, so that was really nice. But when it came time for another pay raise, I was unable to take it because I would have lost my son's insurance, and I could have not afforded the rate to add him. I informed my employer so they kept me one cent under the maximum for two years so that I could keep him insured. At the end of year, I received a bonus instead of the raise in recognition of their appreciation of my work without affecting my benefits.

I knew that God was not satisfied with Shawn and my living arrangements, and I could feel that there were blessings that we were being kept from us because of this. However, marrying him would mean I would lose Caleb's insurance and my tax returns since Shawn was self-employed and behind on his taxes by fifteen thousand dollars still. Logically, the world would say to just stay shacked up, why take a financial loss just to sign some papers? But I could feel that God wanted us to be married. The problem was, as you remember, he didn't want any part of it. So even this was an act of God! The wedding date was set, I let my boss know that I would be open to opportunities once that restriction was gone. I also applied for a very similar job to mine on a whim that was posted with the local community college. It was only a few months after we were married, and I was offered a promotion that more than made up for the insurance premium costs that had changed because we had gotten married. Once again, God had kept his promise.

A few more months later, I got a call to interview for the job with the community college. I had almost forgotten that I had applied for the job; six months had passed. In those six months, I had gotten married and gotten a promotion. I never imagined that if they offered me a job that I would consider leaving a company that had been so good to me for the last two years. I underestimated God's blessing. The offer came in, and it was enough to cover the loss of tax status, the state health insurance was a much lower price, and there was tons of time off up front. I had spoken with my boss about the new offer, and even she could not argue that I should take it. They sent me off with best wishes and gourmet cupcakes. I told them as I left, you never know, maybe they will get me all trained up and I will end up back here.

The new position was grant funded, just as the other had been, but this one at least had a definite end that was three years out. That's was why the pay was good: to attract people to take a risk. So I took the risk. After what I had been through, I knew God was my source, not my job. I got the job, and the pay was what I had been believing God for several years before, making thirty-six thousand a year. The job was great, my supervisor very supportive, and my coworkers on the grant were great mentors. I never intended to continue my education, but working at a college with only a bachelor's degree is rare. I even said at the start, God will just have to keep me here because I am not going back to school. Sometimes God laughs at our plans, you know? A year after being in the job, I started looking at master's degree programs. Luckily since Shawn is a veteran, I was able to get a good rate to attend Liberty University Online.

As the end of the grant neared, it became clear that out of the four of us on the grant, only two would be able to keep positions at the college. Coworkers became competitors, and it was hard. However, I knew I had God's favor in the situation. My supervisor asked for my input on writing the job description, and the people on the interview panel were some of my best supporters in the department. However, I had not finished my degree yet, and the other person had a master's degree and many more years' experience. This was of some concern for me getting the position. But in the end, I got the job and another raise to go with it. Soon after that, I graduated from Liberty University with my master's. Now I have many credentials related to my field and my master's degree.

In only eight years, I have gone from not being able to find my own job to being considered an expert in the field. I had acquired several certifications that allowed me to do contract jobs paying seventy-five dollars per hour to help others after they had been laid off.

Recently, I was approached by the first company that gave me the chance to start in this field to return to a much higher position. They offered me an additional twenty thousand more than what I was making at the time. It seemed really good, and it would also position me within the state as an influencer. However, because of Shawn, I had learned how to hear the voice of God and to follow peace with a decision, and I was not getting any peace with this offer. I disclosed to my current supervisor that even though I had not applied anywhere, there was an opportunity that had been presented to me that I was considering. He did not want to lose me and offered to do anything he could to keep me. I knew the budget was tight and there seemed little chance of getting a raise, but I knew God would work it out. After much consideration and prayer, I told Shawn I just didn't feel right about the offer; God's blessing is where I am now. It just seemed to me that the favor of God surrounded me at my current job. I was spoken highly of, recognized, sought after, and most of all, after the interview for the other position, this was the one I seemed to have peace about. So my supervisor agreed to get me a small raise of about ten percent if I would not take the other job. Weeks passed, and I was waiting to turn the job down, but I had not received a call.

We had gone to court several times around this period, which just seemed like one delay after another, with one ex-

cuse after another. All of this was happening with no promises of ever getting any of the money. At this point, it had been
ten years of delays. My ex had said that it appeared like something was going to go through finally, but only if I signed over
additional custody rights for my son. And if I was not willing
to do this, my son was not going to get a lot of the money that
was promised to him.

I remember considering doing it so that my son would receive the benefits that were promised to him, but something
didn't seem right. So I went and asked Shawn and told him
something didn't sound right, and he told me to call the social
worker that I had been speaking with. Come to find out, my
ex-husband had finally gotten approved for disability and one
of the checks was to be received. He had been doing this to
get access to some of the money before the additional back
check would be distributed. This check was to cover ten years
of missed child support, and I would start to receive month-
ly benefit checks for my son. We agreed to spend some, give
some, and save some. The first check came in one day while I
was at work. I just happened to check my bank account that
day and there was an additional ten thousand dollars in my
account. This was some well needed and desired news that we
had believed God for a long time. Several months later, we received another sizeable check that was three times the amount
of the first one. I wanted to do something special, especially
since my fortieth birthday was approaching. So Shawn and I
decided to take a dream vacation with money we had allotted
to spend. We end up deciding to go on a cruise to the Baha-
mas and Mexico. We added stops before and after to Key West
and Miami. The trip was a dream come true, and it was some-

thing I had believed for a long time.

Usually while we do trips and stuff, Shawn pays for a lot of the recreation things with his commission income, so it was not always super consistent. But this trip he had said that he didn't really have it in his budget, and it would cost him about fifteen hundred dollars in commission over the two weeks we would be gone. We decided to go anyway.

Shawn had told me that he had loved to play blackjack when he used to be in the military. He told me that he was really good, but sadly gambling was not something I liked to do that much. He had told me that he had a rule of one-hundred dollars a day. If he ran out then he stopped. So the first day, we went, we got the one-hundred dollars, and we split the money. We sat down, and I swear in less than twenty minutes, we lost all of our money. I told Shawn that was such a waste. He told me he still liked it anyway, but he did not go down for two more days. There were some other things going on around the cruise ship that consisted of a lot of shopping that Shawn really didn't want to do, so he told me that he was going to play some more blackjack because they had a tournament going on. He went on his merry way, and I went on mine.

About an hour later, I came in to where he was, and he was at the till. He had won nine-hundred dollars. He put three hundred dollars up, and the next day he spent several hundred dollars while we were in Mexico. He had gone a couple of nights later, losing a couple hundred that he had won. But the last night of the cruise, he went down again, and I was expecting him to come for dinner since it was the last night. I really wanted him there and not playing on the table. He said that if he was doing well, he was going to stay but would join as soon as he got done. Well it was about six fifty-five and we typically met some couples that we would have dinner with about seven o'clock every evening. I walked in and he looked white. He was telling me we had to go to the room now! I mean NOW, he would say! Come to find out, he had won an additional fourteen hundred dollars. This was enough money to pay the income he had lost from not working, spending money, and some extra, while having some fun at something he enjoyed.

When we got back from the trip, I got a finally got a call from the company that had offered me the job, but it was not what I had thought. They had lost the contract and the job was no longer going to be filled. I never even had to decline it was like God had only put it there as a route to get me a promotion in my current situation despite budget cuts and layoffs. There have been many things through the years that I have put my faith towards and seen the rewards of my diligence and giving. Losing a job can be a hard and even traumatic experience for many. For those that understand that God has given us promises and desires to fulfill our dreams as well as our needs, it does not have to be. God has used my jobs to teach me to rely on Him and listen for His leading instead of what the world tells me.

A Lesson Learned

Amanda put it best when she said, *"God has used my jobs to teach me to rely on Him and listen for His leading instead of what the world tells me."* Some of the things I remember watching her struggle through are anger and bitterness towards her ex-husband about him and her child support. But she learned not to rely on any of that, not her job, the different positions, the companies, but only God was to be her source! Only God! Also to be clear, I do not play blackjack to gamble, I play it because I love the game! I will play even if no money is involved, just because I love the game. I do it only for fun because it is not my source, God is!

Prayer

Teach me to not rely on anyone but you God! Not my job, spouse, children, child support, the government, the market, the economy, Only You! As I tithe and give, I thank you that you will cause everything my hand touches to prosper because only you are my source!

CHAPTER 54

Vacations

BY 2013, AMANDA AND I had gotten our finances in such a position that we could take vacations, but we had a very limited budget. We had decided that we would go on a vacation only every couple of years so that it did not cause too much strain on the budget. But this year a friend of mine gave me a call that was very involved in our church in the Audio/Video department. I had previously helped him with some basic advice in some real estate deals, and this particular deal was a condo he owned in Myrtle Beach, South Carolina. He called and asked me if we were taking vacation this year.

I informed him that we would probably have to go next year and that it was not really in the budget for this year. He asked if we would want to stay over at his condo near the beach. I asked him how much it would be, and he laughed. He said he was sowing this into my life; he just wanted to be a blessing to us. He said we were an important part in their lives, and they just wanted to thank you us for all we had done. We went down to it, and it was wonderful! It had two bedrooms, two bathrooms, and a kitchen. It was great for a budget. It was so good that we ended up going down and staying there the following year. He even offered us an additional discount, which was such a blessing, even though we had not asked for one. We have been so blessed by this couple and are so grateful for them listening to God and blessing us; we still talk and visit their home as often as we can.

A Lesson Learned

I kept the right attitude about helping people and sowing into their lives. I never tried to get things for free from people. I learned that from David in the Bible. He had an attitude that if there was no sacrifice, then it would not mean as much. I have used these principles in my life and because of it, I have become more and more blessed each year. Even since then, he has invited us to spend much more time with him in his various different properties in the beach area he has owned. I enjoy watching him reach his various passions and enjoy life.

Prayer

Thank you for just one right connection. Thank you for helping the right people, at the right time. I thank you that I can impact people. Let me always be a giver and a sower with my time, talent, and treasure! I will see your mercy, embrace your grace, and thank you for all that you have done in my life!

CHAPTER 55

A Good Man, His Wife
and a Lawn Mower

THERE WAS AN OLDER lady in her fifties named Sabrina that was like a second mother to me. She was a prayer leader at our church, and she was always so faithful to pray for me! And did I need it! The previous years for her had been quite difficult as her husband was diagnosed with a lung condition and only given about six months to live in I believe 2012. He had continued to believe God and against all possibility to beat the verdict the doctors had given him. He was a quick witted and smart man and had been very active before all the problems. I had begun to be more active in pursuing ministry things, and believed I was supposed to go and visit him. Many times over the next several years, I would go and visit him at his home, encourage him in the healing goodness of God, make him laugh, tell jokes, talk about life, and spend time with him.

He had become much softer in his latter days and seemed to have much needed wisdom for all the stupid things I was doing at the time. Many of days I would go over and do most of the talking because he was on ventilation and every breath was a miracle. I cannot speak highly enough of him in this small section of this book, but even though many did not know him, nor would say he had contributed something significant to this world, he contributed a different perspective about the gentleness of a father I had not yet seen at this point in my life. He would tell me to be patient with my boys, learn how to forgive myself, and love with all my heart. In his last few months, I would promise him to quit smoking and I did. I haven't smoked even until today, and this is in part because of my promise to this man! Even in all his trouble in his last days, I never heard him complain. It has served as a reminder that I do not have anything to complain about. He would never give up on God's healing grace, but after several years of fighting a disease, the doctors gave him no chance of surviving. He told his wife he was tired and wanted to go home. She told him yes, and two weeks later he passed away. I was not his child, yet he treated me like a son, something that many in this life may never know!

Over the next several months, I would do whatever I could to help Sabrina do what she needed to. One day she called me up and asked if I knew anything about riding lawn mowers. I told her that I didn't really know much but asked what she needed me to do. She told me that she wanted to fix it and sell it. I asked her how old it was, what condition it was in, and what type it was? Her response was simple. She said she was not really sure, but she knew that it was only ridden about five times, it wasn't that old, but has been sitting around for three years. I asked her how much she wanted for it, and she asked me why I needed a mower. I let her know I had one but might be willing to get another one if it is better than the one I have! Then Sabrina told me she could just give me that one then! I told her she didn't have to, but I thanked her anyway. I went over to her house to get it, and I still had no idea what kind of mower it was! I didn't know if it was working, twenty years old, anything. I had no idea, but I was coming to get it. But when I got over to her house, she took me down to the barn where it had been stored.

It was covered in about two inches of dirt, sawdust, and debris from where it has been sitting. But it looked relatively new. So I got it and took it home. The mower was about five years old and had literally only been ridden about five times before her husband had gotten sick. I cleaned it up, washed it off, changed the gas, plugs, and filters, and it fired right up. It was an automatic, Troy-Bilt® riding mower with a thirty-six to forty-two inch blade. It was in perfect condition. After we got everything cleaned up on it, I took some pictures and sent it back to Sabrina, so she knew it was being taken care of. My wife and I had believed for a newer one. The one we had was old when we got it and then we had it for the last several years. I remember it was burning oil so bad that it would smoke for about ten minutes after I quit riding it.

Now because of my childhood, I didn't like yard work, especially mowing the grass. But God had dealt with me to mow the grass of the people around me. So I would always mow a few extra feet on our neighbor's yards. Sometimes I would even mow the whole yard because they had push mowers. I had been doing this for several years with the expectation that we would get a newer mower. We gave the mower away for free to some neighbors near my dad's house that had some issues before. They would use it two more times before it would quit on them. It must be coincidental that it only ran two times after that. The more amazing thing was that the guy didn't even know how it was still running in the first place; the gas line had melted and fuel was running out almost as fast as it was coming in.

A Lesson Learned

It's been several years since then, and I still have that mower and it still runs great! I still to this day remain in touch with her! She is and has always been such a blessing to me and the body of Christ! She is someone that has prayed for me even in some of my darkest moments and always pointed me to Jesus and the plans he would have for me!

Prayer

I pray that you have people that challenge and inspire you, but I challenge you to pray and inspire others! When you do this, the bible promises for your needs to be met too! But I have learned we have so many more needs then just money! So God, I ask you to meet all my needs, not just my financial, but my emotional, mental, spiritual needs. I know you will because I believe that you will show me how I can love and pray for today!

CHAPTER 56

New Connections

I HAD MET SOMEONE while doing an appraisal one day on a house. We had quite a lengthy conversation with each other. I learned he was a pastor at another church and that he was a volunteer at Roanoke Valley Juvenile Detention Center where he helped troubled youth. He had been involved in that ministry for almost twenty years. I had wanted to get into something like that and had been a youth pastor/minister for the previous three years at that time. But in many cases, I didn't feel that I was really helping the kids at the church I was attending. I finished the appraisal, finished our conversation, exchanged information, and about six months later, I would be working on another house and would see that property as a sale and have to use it as a comparable. I dug out his business card, gave him a call, and we had a lunch. We have been talking ever since. I would soon get connected with him and start volunteering at the detention center with some very good success. In 2015, I would have approximately ten salvations in the six months that I was able to attend.

A Lesson Learned

Over the next several years, we would have over fifty salvations from kids that I would get the opportunity to meet. You never really know that the person you meet today could have an impact on those you meet tomorrow. Make sure that you are always willing to be open to people because you can only bless those by your hands and will be only blessed by others' hands.

Prayer

Lord, teach me to be sensitive to those around me. Help me to learn to give those around me opportunities to help, love, assist, and show compassion. Help me make room for others in my life, and as I do that, let them have an impact around those that I may never meet.

CHAPTER 57

Creation and Crisis

NEAR THE END OF 2015 was a particularly hard year for me. God told me to step back from a lot of different things I was doing at church. He said to begin to prepare for speaking in my own ministry as well as finish several projects that I knew I needed to complete. I went from being a central individual to everyone, to someone that was no longer in the loop. My identity was wrapped up only in what I did for others. I was no longer the "go-to" person, the person that had all the keys, the one in the know, or the one that had the pastor's constant attention. It seemed that almost overnight, I went from the MAN to nobody.

God had to reteach me that my identity was not in what I did, but in who I was in him. This was hard for me because I had been a big worker my entire life, someone that people went to when they needed to get things done. But then I was being told to step back and let others do it. I spent several months severely depressed over this. It seemed that once again things were shifting; I had become the owner of the company and the guy that had been working for me for two years wanted to quit and do something else after all the training I had given him. My dad and I were at some odds because of the split of the company, and the pastor seemed like he wanted nothing to do with me now that I was not so involved. So my question was, who am I when I am not working? These are a few things that I would learn during this period of time.

At the beginning of the year, we started doing some re-cordings on a seminar I called "The Lost Art of Value," which is available for purchase on our website. This business style seminar was approximately fourteen hours long. There was surprisingly more work than I had expected to put into a workshop of this magnitude. It was a very impactful coaching seminar to help people learn to value the things around them such as people, time, and their influence. The five subjects that are discussed are: Knowledge, Numbers, People, Time, and Influence. This was something that I had learned to do over the last several years and thought would be super ben-eficial to others. Many people that I had helped were having some great success.

We finished the recordings at the same time that I was finishing my Masters in Christian Counseling, as well as get-ting my CAYM (Christian Association of Youth Mentors) cer-tification. My dad and I had been at odds about the business and though he had retired, we still continued to work on other investments together. At this point, we had been working on the weekends for the past four years. The property was about eighty percent complete and it just seemed like it was taking forever. The college I was attending at the time was UCML,

and one of the requirements was to write a fifty page the-
sis paper. To the boy that dropped out of high school due to
problems with English, this seemed liked an impossible task.
I first thought of writing the paper on *The Enemies Within –
The Church Killer*, which, after this book, may still be a possibility. I thought I would talk about the gossip, back biting, lack
of leadership, greed, self-interest, lack of love for people, the
cliquey culture, and the atmosphere of religiosity that contra-
dicts most of what I saw in the life of Christ.

I had seen this for over the last ten years in more than just
one church. This was something I knew I could use to help
other churches at a future time. Then I thought about writing it on *Why isn't My Tithe Working - The Five Proofs and Five
Promises in this Covenant* due to of all the kick back about mis-
conceptions that are taught about the Tithe. It had been a very
controversial subject with so many, so I decided to steer from
it for the time being. I thought of doing a paper of my life
and testimonies of God's faithfulness. One morning during
prayer, God gave me the title for this book as I had done my
best to run from God for my entire life. I figured that it would
be the one subject that I might have enough information to
type about. The more I got into it, the more I asked myself,
"how do you turn a subject back off?" Then I realized, I could
maybe make it a short story or a book. Then it was a book,
then a novel because it was over sixty-five thousand words. It
just kept growing and growing. The boy that didn't even pass
high school English is now writing books?

I have continued to speak at Roanoke Valley Juvenile Detention Center when I have the opportunity, which as stated
above would produce many more salvations my second year

with this ministry. Because I was a Gideon, I was able to speak at several other churches about them as well. God had told me that I could begin my own ministry back in 2015, even though I had been in ministry for the past ten years; I had finally been told to GO! I spent the next several months thinking and praying to come up with a name of the ministry, yet nothing was coming to me. But one day after talking with my wife, she suggested that I call it, "Value to Victory!" This has been its name ever since. The focus and mission of it is – Between what you value and your victory is always the cross! This is a simple but profound principle that God has shown me that has revolutionized my life and the lives of those around me. Something I also know will and can change yours!

A Lesson Learned

I don't care who you are, what you have done. If you will simply give God the opportunity to do something in you, he will take your greatest weakness and turn them to strengths. He will teach you to help the helpless and love the unforgiveable. He will mostly show you how to really love and believe in yourself again.

Prayer

Lord, I am willing to be willing. You show me what to do. If you tell me what the next step is, I will take it. For I know that the plans that you have for me are good and for my success and happiness. Because I know that you are a good God, a loving God, full of compassion and wisdom. And I thank you for sharing it with me today.

CHAPTER 58

From the Ashes

MANY PEOPLE THINK THAT when someone hits the spotlight that they came from nowhere, and that there was nothing that they had to deal with. In 2017, I earned my Master's Degree in Christian Counseling from UCML. Yet, considering all of what I came from, it is a miracle that I made it this far. God had encouraged me to go see several counselors and to really work on me. I have seen both Christian and non-Christian counselors and both had some techniques to help me identify and address problems. Counselors, Psychologists, and Psychiatrists, (which I have seen several), have all made different comments about me having or having symptoms of depression, PTSD, ADHD, bi-polar disorder, and being a manic or angry. These are some things that have been said, but one of my psychologists said,

"Of all the things that you have been through, you should be much more messed up than you are". To me, this is a testament of God's grace, not that I have arrived, but that at least

I am making it, making a difference, and that I am changing and allowing God to impact my life and the lives around me. This is something that gives me hope. Something that hopefully will give you hope and encouragement that you are not the only one, that you, no matter what it is, can make it too! The bible says, by the blood of the Lamb and the word of their testimonies, they are saved! My testament will be about the love and grace of God, even when I did it all wrong, he is still a good God, awesome and loving!

A Lesson Learned

I may never reach the standard that some think I should reach. But I will fight, and I will strive to be a better me today! I can give God all the glory for who he is and what he has done in my life.

Prayer

I thank you for all that you are doing in me and through me. I thank you that you have good plans for my life, plans for my success and not for my harm. You have plans to prosper me even as my soul prospers! I pray that I would get more clarity of mind, heart, and soul! No matter how far down I am, I can trade beauty for my ashes!

CHAPTER 59

Count it All Joy

EVEN STILL, AFTER ALL the sexual addiction, pornography, bad relationships, depression, self-harm, poor self-image, drugs, smoking, drinking, bankruptcy, divorce, estrangement from my son and wife, feeling alienated, thoughts of suicide, anger, fighting, and struggles with my sexual orientation, I have realized that I no longer have to *Run from Miracles*. Jesus' continuous, miraculous, overwhelming, miracle-working power has kept me helped through each day. Even now, I'm still on my journey of me *Coming Home* to the miracle maker. He is the one that loves me, helps me, and has kept me!

Having said all of that –

My brethren, count it all joy when you fall into various trials, knowing that the testing of your faith produces patience. But let patience have its perfect work, that you may be perfect and complete, lacking nothing. If any of you lacks wisdom, let him ask of God, who gives to all liberally and without reproach, and it will be given to him. But let him ask in faith, with no doubting, for he who doubts is like a wave of the sea driven and tossed by the wind. For let not that man suppose that he will receive anything from the Lord; he is a double-minded man, unstable in all his ways. (James 1:2-8, NKJV) (NKJV, 1982)

I have learned to be content when I am on the bottom and when I am on the top. I have learned that God is faithful, my defense, and a good God. When we do things His way, we can prosper in every area of our lives. I have learned my addictions, stress, problems, etc. do not minimize his healing power, but expose my lack of willingness to surrender! This is inherently tied to my own unwillingness to give up my personal desires.

It seems to me that much of my life, the things that I was dreading, resenting, expecting or even hoping for never worked out the way I was expecting. Sometimes the process is not what we expect, but it what can change our life. As you read my story, I hope that you saw my despair, hope, pain, passion, and purpose. I hope you can relate them to your life, situations, and circumstances. See that it is the little things and moments that change you and your life; many times, the miracle is in the moment and the detail.

What things in your life have you been running from? Are there certain joys, pains, failures, or passions you have begun to run from because of previous situations? What is something you are being challenged to change that you know would impact your life, but you're not quite sure how to go about it?

Sometimes we have done things in our lives just to survive, not that it is right or God, but what we thought we had to do it at the time. There are so many different examples in the

Bible where people did things to survive that were not right. God corrected them for that. Instead, he says to repent and turn to him. This means to turn to his way of doing things, not just what you think is the "right way", but the God way. I assure, you there is a big difference. Sometimes our miracle in life is God's sustaining power that we just simply survived.

I now have a good marriage, a good relationship with my son and step-son, my parents, my father, and step-sister. I now have good friends that are there for me, even after my lowest points. When you have lost and given up on everything, but can look around and still you have people, you are blessed.

I have been successful in business, making over six figures at the time of writing this book, and expect to make even more. God has blessed me to have been able to give to charities, organizations, and people wherever I go. We were able to partner with both the Roanoke Rescue Mission and Hunters for Hungry, being able to deliver over ten thousand pounds of deer meat, feeding twenty-five thousand people.

Because of the problems that I have dealt with, I have been given a unique perspective on relationships and the effects of them on my mind. I have seen that, even when we do things the wrong way, we still can see the power of God. God was doing His absolute best to guide us through, despite us getting in our own way. I am so happy that God has never given up on me and has always been a faithful friend and companion, even when I didn't know He was by my side. I know that he is wanting to come along and guide you. I hope to encourage you that, no matter what you are going through, God is the answer! He will always bring you through. Stop running from God, the miracle maker, and realize that you have been *Run-*

ning from Miracles and It's Time to Come Home!

God is still working, and I am still seeing miracles, even while I have been writing and attempting to finish this book. I have seen levels of breakthrough in my finances, marriage, family and friends. I look forward to seeing you and encouraging you in your walk with Christ.

Lesson Learned

As I close this book, I would like to say that no matter how low you go there is still a way out. God never promised us a life without struggles but did promise that we would be overcomers. Which means there are things in life we have to come over. So hopefully all the things that I have gone through encourage you to know that you can overcome every situation in your life. That just because you don't do everything right, it does not change that God has a everlasting love towards you. That His mercy is renewed every morning. That He is faithful and has a love that will never change. That He is the perfect father wanting a relationship with you in your every day life. So just because you have been knocked down, it doesn't mean you are out for the count. Make sure you remember, your referee is the same person that died on the cross, defeated hell and the grave. He came back with the keys of life so you could have a life of victory.

Prayer

I pray that whoever has read this book, that it provides hope and a desire to know the God I have learned to love. That He will become your trusted guide, friend, confidant, companion, father, healer, provider and counselor. I pray that your hope does not fail you, that you rise above every storm, and know that no matter how dark things appear, that the light of God can live in us! That I am a lamp set on a hill, to help those all around me, even in the middle of whatever I may be going through right this very second. So no matter what, I will give God all the glory and all the praise for He is the reason in which I have hope. In Jesus Name, Amen!

Bonus Chapter:
The Blessing Jar

WE HAVE A LARGE glass jar that we call the "blessing jar." Every time we notice God's blessing on our lives, we take a piece of paper and jot down what happened and place it into the jar. At the end of the year, New Year's Eve, we try to review these slips to remind us of all the things we should thank God for. A few of the stories in this book were slips of paper at one time. This year has been no different; there are many things to be thankful for that many would call luck or coincidence. We recognize that they are miracles and blessings that belong in that jar. Hopefully this tradition will help you to look for and recognize God's presence in your life.

Just a few weeks ago, while I was speaking with my son Cameron, he told me that his physician said that his case of Crohn's has gone from what was one of the worst that they had seen, requiring eighteen pills at one point, to now no longer needing any pills and only one shot a month. Caleb, my other son, skipped tenth grade, going from being a freshman to a junior. This was done by his planning and foresight. We also:

- Sold a property that we were upside down on without losing money.
- Bought a new home that we were able to completely renovate.
- While purchasing our home, we also got a second property for one dollar that we purchased with change.
- Two major promotions for Amanda at work.
- Improved marriage to a new level.
- Best relationship between my Dad and I that I have ever had. We talk almost every day.
- Went on several cruise vacations that I had never been on as an adult.
- Was picked up by a publishing company for this book.

There is no end to his mercy, compassion, love, and grace! My desire was to instill hope in your life from a loving God. I also wanted to tell you a little about the Jesus I serve and know! I am far from perfect, but if you would like to meet Christ today, please just say the prayer below and I am sure he will come to meet you right where you are so you can begin your life with him today.

CHAPTER 61

Salvation Prayer

I DO NOT BELIEVE that it is an accident that you have chosen this book. If you have not met Christ as your personal savior, I would like to give you the opportunity to say a simple prayer that is backed from God's word. Just simply speak this little prayer and meet a father of unconditional love! Come meet the Jesus I have come to love!

Heavenly Father, I come to you right now, a sinner, in need of a savior. Thank you Jesus for dying for my sins. I believe that God raised you from the dead, and that I've been set free. I accept your mercy, I embrace Grace, and I am choosing today to follow you for the rest of my life.

Written by Dustin Stradley

Now that you have done this, we would love for you to get in touch with us so that we can get some additional resources in your hand and help you along in your journey. Please visit us at www.shawnedecker.com so that we can do so today. Let others know how we are helping people all around the world, just like you! You are so very important to us!

We hope to hear from you soon and how we are impacting your life! If you would like to give a testimony about something God has done in your life, please email us at valuetovictory@gmail.com and in the subject line just simply put *Testimony RFM*, and let us know all that God is doing!

More Traditional Salvation Prayer

IF YOU DO NOT know Jesus as your Savior and Lord, simply pray the following prayer in faith and Jesus will be your Lord!

Heavenly Father, I come to You in the Name of Jesus. Your Word says, "Whosoever shall call on the name of the Lord shall be saved" (Acts 2:21). I am calling on You. I pray and ask Jesus to come into my heart and be Lord over my life according to Romans 10:9-10: "If thou shalt confess with thy mouth the Lord Jesus, and shalt believe in thine heart that God has raised him from the dead, thou shalt be saved. For with the heart man believeth unto righteousness; and with the mouth confession is made unto salvation." I do that now. I confess that Jesus is Lord, and I believe in my heart that God raised Him from the dead.

I am now reborn! I am a Christian—a child of Almighty God!

I am saved! You also said in Your Word, "If ye then being evil, know how to give good gifts unto your children: HOW MUCH MORE shall your heavenly Father give the Holy Spirit to them that ask him?" (Luke 11:13). I'm also asking You to fill me with the Holy Spirit. Holy Spirit, rise up within me as I praise God. I fully expect to speak with other tongues as You give me the utterance (Acts 2:4). In Jesus' Name. Amen.

If this book or ministry has helped you or a loved one and you would like to partner with us, we would love to have you! We thank you and hope that you have been blessed, inspired, and encouraged! For more information, visit our website ShawnEDecker.com or ValuetoVictory.com

Works Cited

Communities, H. (2000, 01 01). *Health Communities.* Retrieved from http://www.healthcommunities.com/bells-palsy/overview-of-bells-palsy.shtml

Consecration Conference. (2007). Retrieved from PR Leap: http://www.prleap.com/pr/74192/life-coach-paula-white-to-keynote-jamestown "(PRLEAP.COM)

NKJV. (1982). The Holy Bible, NKJV. Nashville, TN: Thomas Nelson.

Wiki. (n.d.). *Wikipedia.* Retrieved from https://en.wikipedia.org/wiki/Bell%27s_palsy